'He made authentic music and proved that you can be Irish and still play the Blues.'
DAVY SPILLANE, UILEANN PIPER

'He was the first international rock star from Ireland and he set a great example.'
PAUL MCGUINNESS, MANAGER OF U2

'Rory's death really upset me, I heard about it just before we went on stage and it put a dampener on the evening. I can't say that I knew him that well but I remember meeting him in our offices once and we spent an hour talking, he was such a nice guy and a great player.' **JIMMY PAGE, LED ZEPPELIN**

'He was such a purist, he wouldn't sell himself out. How many people do you know of in the music business who would take that kind of stand? If there weren't people like Rory Gallagher around to set that kind of example, then it would probably spell the end of quality music.' **GARY MOORE**

Rory Gallagher and Phil Lynott, Punchestown, 1982. (© Colm Henry)

Rory with his treasured mandolin, performing 'Goin' to My Home Town' in Manchester in 1979 (courtesy Steve Smith).

MARCUS CONNAUGHTON

RORY GALLAGHER

His Life and Times

The Collins Press

FIRST PUBLISHED IN PAPERBACK IN 2014 by
The Collins Press
West Link Park
Doughcloyne
Wilton
Cork

First published in hardback 2012

© Marcus Connaughton 2012

Marcus Connaughton has asserted his moral right to be identified as the author of this work in accordance with the Copyright and Related Rights Act 2000.

A CIP record for this book is available from the British Library.

Paperback ISBN-13: 9781848892187
Hardback ISBN-13: 9781848891531
EPUB eBook ISBN: 9781848899803
PDG eBook ISBN: 9781848899803
mobi eBook ISBN: 9781848899810

Design and typesetting by Burns Design
Typeset in Walbaum and Franklin Gothic

Printed in Poland by Białostockie Zakłady Graficzne SA

CONTENTS

'Blues is an affirmation of the Spirit, a howl of pain, a bawdy punchline, a railing against injustice, a longing for peace and rest, a prayer for salvation, an ode to a household, a poem of regret, a boast of prowess, a family portrait, a celebration of love, a junkies lament, a documentary of a juke joint stabbing, a tale of life lived on the highway, an open letter to God or to Satan. Blues is subtle, brutal, ecstatic, mournful. It is music of the soil, of the street, of the heart. It is deceptively simple in structure, boundless in expressiveness. It is guitar music by and large, from the ghostly acoustic wailings of Robert Johnson to the electrified shootouts of countless bar room guitar slingers over half a century later.'

TOM WHEELER, GUITAR PLAYER MAGAZINE, APRIL 1990

Rory in City Hall, Cork, in the 1980s. (courtesy *Irish Examiner* Publications)

Rory

HALLA NA CATHRACH, CORCAIGH 1976
Louis de Paor

Milliún míle siar uait
Thiar I dtóin an halla
Bhí mo chroí ag bualadh
Tiompán mo bhas,
An chruit im chuisle á míniú amach,
Idir t'ordóg is m'inchinn bhuailte,
Gan nóta im cheann
Ach an spionnadh a chuiris-se
le sreanganna in achrann.

B'ait lion go ragfá ag tincéireacht
Mar sin ar bhuile scoir an tiúin
Is tormán ár mbasbhualaidh
Ag líonadh fé shála do lámh
A thug snámh smigín dom mhian
Ag trácht ar uisce coipthe.

An é nár airís an tuile
Ag líonadh ort,rabharta cos is lámh
A dhein bord loinge den urlár
i Halla na Cathrach
is ná líonfaidh feasta an poll
a d'fhágais ar ardán id dhiadh?

An mbraitheann tú anois é
Ár ngile mearluaimneach méar,
Is solas na bhflaitheas
Ag sluaistiú ciúnais
Ar shúile an tslua
Atá buailte le stáitse
Ag glaoch ar ais ort ón ndoircheacht:

Rory
Rory
Rory
An gcloiseann tú anois ár nguí?

Rory

CORK CITY HALL 1976
Louis de Paor

A million miles away from you
Right at the back of the hall
My heart was beating
The drums of my hands;
I hadn't a note in my head
Only the grace notes you picked
From tangled strings
As the knot in my veins
Was undone by your brilliant fingers.

I couldn't work out
Why you kept tinkering
With the end of the tune
While the roar of our applause
Rose up under the heels of your hands
That kept my dreams above water
As you walked the angry sea.

Did you really not hear
The tide flooding in behind you,
The waves of pounding feet
That rocked the floor of the City Hall
Until it rolled like the deck of a ship,
That will never fill the emptiness
You left behind you on stage?

Can you feel it now,
Our swiftfingered brightness
As the light of heaven
Shovels silence
On the eyes of the crowd
As they press against the stage,
Calling you back from the dark:

Rory
Rory
Rory
Now can you hear me?

Rory plays his beloved Stratocaster. He bought it second-hand on hire purchase from Crowley's Music Centre in Cork in 1963. (© Fin Costello)

1
The Fender
Stratocaster

RORY GALLAGHER was a fifteen-year-old schoolboy in Cork when he first laid hands on the guitar that would be associated with him for the rest of his life. The year was 1963 and the guitar was a 1961 Fender Stratocaster (Sunburst Model). Rory bought it second-hand on hire purchase, for £100 – then an extremely large sum. He had been inspired in his choice of instrument by Buddy Holly, who first popularised the Strat in America.

Michael Crowley, late proprietor of Crowley's Music Centre in Cork, remembered the young musician visiting his shop on Merchants Quay, right on the banks of the River Lee. There was a new Stratocaster in the window. 'Rory called in with his mother, who asked what price was the guitar? Including the case at the time, they were £129.

Michael Crowley (right) pictured with Seamus 'Seamie' Long in Crowley's Music Centre on Merchants Quay, Cork, in the 1960s. (Courtesy Sheena Crowley, Crowleys Music Centre).

When she heard the price, she said to Rory, "That's rather expensive, like, would anything else do?" We had a man working here at the time, his name was Seamus Long. Seamus was a great salesman and he interjected and said, "How about one of the Hagstroms?" Rory shook his head and said, "No!" He was only fifteen, which was very young for somebody to be into a guitar of that type, but he obviously knew what he wanted and had probably read a whole lot more about them than I had. He was obviously aware that a lot of the players in the United States were using them.'

Designed in 1954 by the world famous Fender Musical Instruments Corporation, the Stratocaster 'looked like something out of Buck Rogers' with its 'horns, body contours, glossy finish and flash gadgetry'. A lot musicians actually 'shied away from the new instrument' when they first saw it, wrote the authors of *Curves, Contours and Body Horns: The Story of the Fender Stratocaster*. 'It was so new-fangled few could see themselves playing it.' Buddy Holly was an exception to the rule, and his first album, *The Chirping Crickets*, was a milestone for the Strat. 'The album cover, which showed Holly holding his early

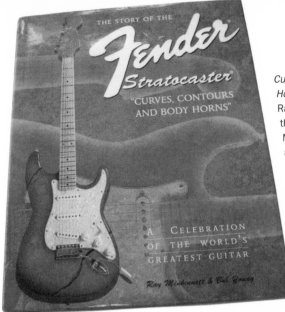

Curves, Contours and Body Horns written by guitarist Ray Minhinnett (who gave the second Rory Gallagher Memorial Lecture in 1996 at the Cork Institute of Technology Arts Festival) and charting the story of Leo Fender and the Fender guitar, and those who played them, including Rory Gallagher.

Sunburst Strat, was the best piece of publicity the company could have asked for, and for a huge number of players, including Hank Marvin, Eric Clapton, Jeff Beck, and Rory Gallagher, this was the first time they had seen the new instrument. The excitement wasn't only visual, for Holly popularised the sound of the small rock and roll combo – guitar, vocals, bass and drums – which would become the standard for rock music.'

Michael Crowley had sold only two Strats prior to Rory showing an interest in the guitar. The first had gone to Jim Conlon of the Royal Showband in Waterford. Conlon liked the guitar but had to return it when the Royal Showband decided to change their uniforms. The Sunburst Strat did not match the new salmon-pink colours of the band, and so it was sent back to the music store in Cork, travelling up from Waterford as cargo in the back of a bus. Michael Crowley had promised Rory's mother that he would let her know if he ever got a second-hand Strat, and so he went straight up to their home on MacCurtain Street. 'I think that was around twelve o'clock in the morning. When we reopened at two, Rory was there, standing at the door. He came in and looked at the guitar. I offered it to him and he just held it in his hand and said "Yeah, that's it!" and ran off up home.'

A lot of tourists to Cork still call by Crowley's Music Centre, which has since relocated to MacCurtain Street. It is a place of pilgrimage for fans and has a wall plaque dedicated to Rory Gallagher. They want to discover the story behind the famous guitar. 'It's a regular happening, there isn't a week that would go by that we'd have somebody in. There have been people from Australia, Japan and America. Also a very great number of German, Dutch, and French people, Scandinavians too. Rory was very, very popular on the continent and very well liked there.'

'MacCurtain Street was Rory's backyard,' recalled Michael Crowley, 'and I can remember that he went to school around the corner at St Kieran's College, Camden Quay. I had an uncle living in Blackpool at the time and occasionally, on my way back from him, I would come along Camden Quay. I remember on one occasion Rory was sitting on the steps outside. It was a bit after school starting back – about a quarter past two. He appeared not too keen on going in. I spoke to him for a while and you could see with Rory that his heart was elsewhere. He was anxious to get home to play some music.' Michael Crowley was surprised at how good Rory was when he finally heard him, practising with a showband called Fontana in the Gaiety Ballroom in Oliver Plunkett Street. 'It was a complete surprise, the standard that he had reached. Knowing everybody else at the time and, ye'know, the way they would struggle with fairly simple tunes, he was obviously a unique talent.'

Rory came from a musical family. His father, Daniel, played the accordion and sang with the Tir Chonaill Ceili Band in Ballyshannon in Donegal while his mother, Monica, acted and sang. Rory was born on 2 March 1948 in the appropriately named Rock Hospital in Ballyshannon. His parents, from Derry and Cork respectively, had moved there when Daniel secured work on the Erne hydro-electric scheme. Ireland was on the cusp of declaring itself a republic and the rural electrification scheme was in full flight; Donegal and Kerry were the last two counties to be connected to the national grid. Rory's parents had met when Daniel was in the army and stationed in Cork. Monica, a Roche by birth, was the daughter of a publican on MacCurtain Street. In 1949, the family moved to Derry and it was here that Rory's brother Donal was born. Monica moved back to Cork with the boys in 1958. They lived at first with their grandmother on MacCurtain Street, right in the heart of the city. Rory attended the North Monastery School at first, appearing on the school roll-book as Ruairí Ó Gallchoir. He later moved to St Kieran's College on Camden Quay where he prospered after the more repressed regime of the North Mon.

'Puttin' on the Style' – Rory in studio with one of his boyhood idols Lonnie Donegan, king of skiffle.

Guitars were something of a rarity in late 1950s Ireland. Rory was hooked, however, the first time he saw one. He played at first with a round cheese box with a ruler and some elastic bands, in much the same way that American bluesmen had used cigar boxes with porch screen wire. He then acquired a simple guitar from Woolworths. Rory's mother supported his interest in music from a young age and secured his first acoustic guitar by mail order in 1957 while the family was still living in Derry. She got it through William Doherty, who was an agent for *Kay & Co. of Glasgow*. Many years earlier in the Mississippi Delta, a musician named McKinley Morganfield (better known as Muddy Waters) secured his first acoustic guitar through a similar Sears catalogue.

Rory was a capable musician from an early age and it was all natural. 'Although my entire family are musical – and my early life was spent performing at family parties and that sort of gathering – I only play by ear,' he said. 'I've never had any musical training at all.' Speaking to Colm Keane for a documentary on RTÉ Radio 1, Rory described how he 'found material from the late 1950s and early 1960s in the pages of songbooks like Lonnie Donegan's *Skiffle Hits*, which had small chord symbols and diagrams to go with the songs. So I just put that together and started digging out a few chords and

5

learning all the songs that Lonnie was doing. Most of the material was Woody Guthrie stuff or Leadbelly, so it was a good second-hand way of discovering these American songs. And then you had, at the time, those Fats Domino and Chuck Berry songs ... you'd just learn everything you could within reason and that's more or less how I started. It's almost like teach yourself and, you know, discover for yourself from the radio.'

According to his brother, Rory went to the Cork School of Music to look for lessons but there were none on offer. Strange as it sounds today, guitar lessons only began there in the early 1970s. Rory did get some help tuning his guitars from James O'Brien, a neighbour who ran O'Brien's Ice Cream Parlour on MacCurtain Street. Just as importantly, O'Brien was the Classical Guitar correspondent for *Banjo, Mandolin and Guitar* (*BMG*) magazine, in whose pages Rory discovered some of the African-American bluesmen like Leadbelly and Big Bill Broonzy that were to inspire him right to the time of his passing. The July 1959 issue, for example, carried a photo of Josh White who was to play London that summer. Priced at one shilling and sixpence, *BMG* declared itself as the 'Oldest Established and Most Widely Read Fretted Instrument Magazine in the World'. Rory settled on the type of amplification he would use through *BMG* – the famous

The July 1959 issue of *Banjo, Mandolin and Guitar* magazine. James O'Brien, a neighbour of the Gallagher family, was Classical Guitar correspondent for the magazine and helped Rory to tune his guitars.

This VOX advertisement appeared in *Banjo, Mandolin and Guitar* magazine. The VOX amplifier was Rory's amp of choice. The fact that it was also used by Liverpool's The Big Three, of whom he was a major fan, influenced his decision.

VOX AC 30. Speaking in later years, Rory said 'I still use the old VOX AC 30 that I carried about with me for six years with Taste. It's a great amp and it gives me so much power.'

The Strat, however, was the key to Rory's sound. He could talk about it all night. 'It's dated November 1961 – in certain people's opinions this is when Fender hit their peak. I like the maple neck. Like on the earlier guitars, they're probably a bit more crisp, but there's a warmth to this, a mellowness because of the rosewood neck. This is the best, it's my life, this is my best friend. It's almost like knowing its weak spots are strong spots. I don't like to get sentimental about these things, but when you spend thirty years of your life with the same instrument it's like a walking memory bank of your life there in your arms.

'I've always wanted to get that Gibson sustain out of my Fender. I've borrowed Gibsons and tried them; you can get the sustain but you can never get that clarity of sound that you get with the Strat. The controls seem all wrong to me on a Gibson as well, when I play one I'm looking for the controls and I discover that they are way below my hand and that I'm lifting the guitar up to reach the controls. I like to get that sort of phase sound by using the volume swell on the Stratocaster ... and that's impossible on a Gibson.

'I'm using Fender Rock and Roll strings. I've been with them for some time because you can get them easily anywhere in the world

David Foley, a Gallagher fan, and Michael Crowley with David's Signature Fender Stratocaster, one of the guitars produced to represent Rory's favourite guitar.

and they perform very well. I've tried Ernie Ball strings and I used Clifford Essex strings for quite some time, but I'm fairly settled with Fenders.

'I'm amazed that despite its age I've never even had to adjust the truss rod, I've taken it to some of the hottest countries in the world and it just never moves. It's great. I've had it re-fretted a couple of times but apart from that very little has been done. I had it stolen one time, following a brief appearance at the Five Club to visit Pat Egan about the Dublin scene, and it got very beaten up then. I had borrowed a Telecaster, and it and the Tele were nicked. I was terrified for a few days in case I would have to buy both a Strat and a Telecaster. Both guitars were found (with the assistance of some exposure on *Garda Patrol* on RTÉ) behind a front garden wall on the South Circular Road, with some of the strings missing and the bodies knocked about but, thankfully, they were ok.

'People look at my guitar and think that I must treat it badly. I admit I used to throw it about a bit in the early days, but it's really just that I use it so much that, over the years, the paint has gone, one little chip at a time. I don't see guitars as things to be left in glass cases. I love all great guitars, but they have to be used and I can get a kick out of a $15 dollar Silvertone too. It's not meanness; it's just that any guitar over x-hundred pounds just becomes a status symbol. Then again, I grew up in a time when I remember Telecasters and Stratocasters being £100 or £200, whatever.

'This guitar is part of my psychic make-up. I've had troubles with it but I'm fortunate enough. It's like B.B. King has a hundred Lucille's; I've only got one Strat. I don't even call it a woman's name or whatever: it's just where I came from, to own a Stratocaster was like monumental – it was impossible. There'll be arch battles for as long as we go on about the warmth of Les Paul guitars and the twang of a Telecaster and all that, but I would panic before I go on stage without this guitar – it would have to be a Strat and this one in particular.'

2

The Scene

This photo of Rory was taken after school in St Kieran's College, Cork. Here he is sporting the school scarf, which was knitted by 'Irish' Jack Lyons' mother (courtesy Jack Lyons).

HE YOUNG RORY GALLAGHER would try to get his hands on everything to do with music that came into Cork city. Pigotts on Patrick's Street, which sold pianos and sheet music, was one of his favourite haunts from the time he was twelve. Ursula's Record Store on Oliver Plunkett Street was another. These shops carried a limited stock of chart and back catalogue material, a far call from iTunes but with much more personal contact and the added thrill of being able to touch and feel that sleeve and examine the pristine vinyl.

Fitzgerald's electrical store on the Grand Parade also carried a small selection of records. The record retail industry was in its infancy and, although many people today will find it difficult to believe, electrical and hardware stores in many of the major towns and cities carried a stock of chart singles and some albums in the corner, the equivalent of loose biscuits in the grocery shops of the time. A lot depended on the enthusiasm of the shop staff and the musical tastes of whoever had purchasing power. In my own case, the store sold bicycles and electrical goods. I bought my first four albums in McHugh Himself under the railway bridge on Talbot Street in Dublin. The albums were *Taste* – Taste, *Revolver* – The Beatles, *D'Israeli Gears* – Cream, and *King of the Delta Blues Singers* – Robert Johnson. Not a bad start for a boy growing up on Dublin's northside.

Sheila MacCurtain, the buyer in Eason's, was a doyenne of the fledgling record retailing industry, and if she was aware of a customer's specific tastes she would seek them out. Sheila, the daughter of Tomás MacCurtain, Republican hero and former Lord Mayor of Cork, later ran the record division in Eason's on Patrick's Street where many Gallagher fans in the early 1970s bought their first Gallagher vinyl. Elsewhere around the country, you had Prims in Kilkenny. In Dublin you had Discfinder on Baggot Street, Liam Breen's on Liffey Street, and Pat Egan's Sound Cellar on Nassau Street. The latter still thrives today with the avuncular and ever-helpful Tommy Tighe. The Sound Cellar has survived through Tommy's unique personal service, whether for fans of roots, blues, alt-country or metal in whatever form.

The first records that Rory bought in Cork were most likely Lonnie Donegan's *Rock Island Line* and the *Buddy Holly Story* in Ursula's. Donegan was at the vanguard of the British skiffle movement, which was the bridge for many young musicians of the late 1950s into popular music and rock and roll. At one time in the 1950s there were thousands of skiffle bands throughout Britain, although it never really took off

Rory was a fan of The Big Three from Liverpool. Here is the front cover of their EP *At the Cavern*.

The Boy Who Dared To Rock – The Definitive Elvis by Paul Lichter, shows Elvis Presley, who was a great inspiration for Rory – his first guitar (bought from Woolworths) featured the King. In 1992 Rory was admitted into the Fender Hall of Fame, joining his hero and Elvis guitarist – James Burton.

to the same degree here. Rory, through listening to Donegan, went after the source, discovering Jesse Fuller, Huddie Leadbetter, better known as Leadbelly, and Woody Guthrie – the great American folk poet and troubadour. Later he was to make his version of Leadbelly's 'Out on the Western Plain' an anthem for fans of acoustic blues.

Coming across a copy of an EP (extended play) single by The Big Three from Liverpool was certainly another turning point for Rory. The single was released in 1963 featuring three cover versions – Ray Charles' 'What'd I Say', 'Reelin' and a Rockin' by Chuck Berry, and 'Zip A Dee-Doo Dah' by Wrubel & Gilbert – and one original by the three piece called 'Don't Start Running Away'. The Big Three were Johnny Hutchinson on drums, Johnny Gustafson on bass guitar, and Brian Griffiths on lead guitar. Gallagher's other early heroes included Larry Williams, Chuck Berry, Eddie Cochran, Elvis Presley, Buddy Holly, Gene Vincent, Jimmy Reed, and the Buddha of the blues – Muddy

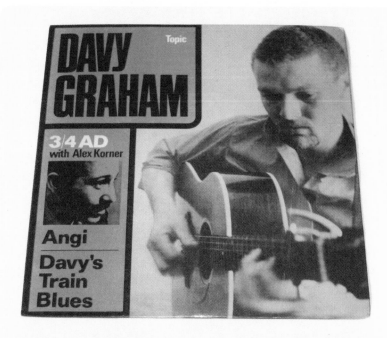

Davy Graham is the guitarist who is widely credited with creating the DADGAD chord format for acoustic guitar. His playing of 'Angi' was a target to be mastered by all aspiring guitarists in the 1960s. Graham wrote 'Angi' when he was nineteen years old and it was released on his debut EP in 1962. Rory acknowledged Davy, the late Bert Jansch and the encouragement of Alexis Korner as major influences on his acoustic playing.

Waters. The young Cork teenager discovered photographs of his idols in magazines like *Melody Maker* and *New Musical Express*. In just a few years, Rory was to feature on their front pages.

Pat Egan, the pioneering independent record retailer, is one of the pivotal figures in the history of Irish popular culture, alongside concert promoter Jim Aiken. His Beat Column in *Spotlight* magazine and its successors was one of the few ways of learning about exciting new bands in the early 1960s when there was no pop radio in Ireland. Egan, also a popular club DJ, kept his ear to the ground so that line-up changes, which were almost a weekly occurrence, could be charted and followed by the growing fan base for this exciting alternative music. He encouraged emerging beat and rock groups at every turn and was central to propagating and rallying the emergence of Rory Gallagher throughout those early Taste days and into his solo career.

The centre of the beat universe in Cork was the Cavern Club, later to become the 006, behind what is now CP Tronix on Leitrim Street. Here the visiting groups performed in a ramshackle timber building, which, during the summer of 1966, had visits from John Mayall and the Bluesbreakers, Gary Moore, and The Creatures. Entry was by presentation of your blue membership card through the archway with the splintered mirror inset beside the cramped ticket desk. Nearby, the Munster Hotel housed the Hilton – The Students Club while further along MacCurtain Street was the Crypt, which featured raw young talent. Bigger places like the Arcadia were sown up by the showbands.

When I moved to Rory's home town in 1994 I spoke to Mick Leary who recalled that, during that time in the 1960s, he would stand outside the Savoy with an album cover in his hand hoping some like-minded soul would approach to talk music. 'Look at this album I've got. Would you know about this band?' This was happening in towns and cities throughout Ireland but there was a wonderful intimacy and spirit in a city like Cork with the hills converging and everyone drifting down into town at the weekends, meeting on Patrick's Street and MacCurtain Street to engage with what was on offer.

Who had heard what on the radio was another question often asked, this being the era of the pirate radio stations and the American Forces Network. In the late 1950s and early 1960s the American Forces Network broadcast the music taking the United States by storm to the troops still serving in Europe, including Belfast. Music fans throughout Europe were able to hear, for the first time, Buddy Holly, Carl Perkins, Little Richard, Muddy Waters, and Elvis Presley by moving the dial to the appropriate position on the crackling valve radio.

Radio Luxembourg's English language service, FAB 208, was another important source. We listened to Luxembourg at that time with a bicycle lamp under the bedclothes when transistor radios were the size of shoe boxes – our favourite being the art deco style Bush model. Most households at the time had no television and the radio was more than likely a Pye model with those valves that took a short while to warm up. Both FAB 208 and Radio Caroline, the pirate radio station started by Irishman Ronan O'Rahilly in March 1964, were to change the face of broadcasting and popular music and culture with seismic effect, blasting the latest pop tunes into homes throughout

Europe. In September 1967, the BBC responded by starting their own popular music service, BBC Radio 1. In the process they hired many of the DJs who had established themselves on either FAB 208 or the pirates, including Jimmy Saville, Noel Edmonds, and Tony Blackburn. Van Morisson, like Rory, was an avid listener, and he refers to all these stations in a number of songs, 'The Days Before Rock and Roll' being just one example.

First of the NEW WAVE—

IMPACT
Showband CORK

Rare images of the Fontana Showband and Impact, which are held by Philip Prendergast's widow, Sarah.

THE MAJORITY OF young musicians in the early to mid-1960s found it hard to get regular work and so, exasperated, they joined showbands with their strict dress codes. Rory was no exception. 'I tried to get a beat group together and the only groups around I think were Van Morrison and Them in Belfast and a few in Dublin like The Creatures, The Others, The Orange Machine and a few bands like that. But in Cork you would still find it hard to find a bass guitarist, the odd drummer alright would be around but most musicians decided if they got a job with a dance band at least you got paid for doing that, whereas with a beat group you had to "pay to play" nearly. But like when you're fifteen or something you're quite happy to put up with a few hours with a showband just to get away and see other places, and plus part of the show you'd enjoy doing anyway; you'd be doing rock and roll standards like "Slow It Down" and so on. Eventually it [the showband circuit] would just eat you up, and you'd just decide you're getting claustrophobia there and you had to do or die and actually start a band properly.'

The Irish showband was a somewhat unique ensemble of musicians emerging from the end of large-scale dance bands in the 1950s such as Mick Delahunty and Ambrose Walsh and Jack Ruane. Many consider that the showband era began with the Clipper Carlton. Musician Dave Glover is widely credited as coining the term 'showband', distinguished by the inclusion of brass players in the line-ups and the fact that these musicians presented a show with other entertainment on stage during the performances. Northern Ireland was a bedrock of those musicians who crossed over and had a major influence on the development of the ballroom circuit in the south. These ballrooms, which were usually located at crossroads in remote rural locations, were primitive affairs, with no changing rooms and could generally accommodate over a thousand couples.

The premier showband venue and dance hall in Cork city was the Arcadia, opposite Kent Railway Station. Here, The Dixies led the charge fronted by Brendan O'Brien and the irrepressible Joe MacCarthy on the drums. On the main Dublin to Cork road for many years a sign welcomed you to 'Cork – Home of The Dixies'. While the showbands played the cities, their main touring haunts were the major rural ballrooms such as Red Barn in Youghal. The Royal Showband were regular visitors to the Majorca and the Pinewood, with special buses laid on from the city. These showbands played covers of hit material and Gallagher saw the opportunity to get some experience on the road after school.

In 1963, aged fifteen, Rory joined the Fontana Showband in Cork (there was another Fontana based in Dunloy in County Antrim and formed from an outfit called the Teenbeats). He stayed with them for almost two years. The Fontana were Bernie Tobin on trombone, his brother Oliver on bass guitar, Declan O'Keefe on rhythm guitar, Rory on lead guitar, John Lehane on saxophone, and Eamonn O'Sullivan on drums. A year later, with a name change to reflect a more rock-influenced set list, the band became The Impact, adding Michael Lehane on keyboards and Johnny Campbell replacing O'Sullivan behind the drum kit.

In April 2012 Cork musician and guitarist Tim O'Leary revealed a treasury of rare and previously unseen Fontana memorabilia which had been accumulated by the former manager of the showband, Philip Prendergast, from 1963 to 1965. Many of the photographs were taken in Jacques Photographic Studio on Oliver Plunkett Street, Cork.

Philip Prendergast's widow, Sarah, discovered the material during a house move and over two years ago passed the material to family

friend Tim. Tim hopes to find a suitable permanent home for these important items in either a proposed Gallagher Archive or the Rory Gallagher Music Library.

Unique amongst the collection are early publicity stills which show Rory's famed Fender Strato-caster in pristine condition and his first passport photo taken in the photo booth of Woolworth's in Cork in 1964. Also in the cache of treasured items is a quarter inch tape recording from 1964, still in mint condition at seven and a half inches per second, recorded

Rory about to catch a flight to Spain in 1964 after finishing school in St Kieran's College. Rory gave this photo to fan John Byrne (courtesy John Byrne).

in Kingsway Studios in London with Rory Gallagher playing on all tracks and taking the lead on vocals and guitar on the classic 'Slow Down' by Larry Williams. Williams, an R&B favourite of Rory and John Lennon, also wrote 'Bony Marony'. Another song on this rare tape is 'My Bonnie Lies Over the Ocean'.

When the Plattermen, originally The Platters Showband, with Arty McGlynn on guitar played the Arcadia in 1965 the relief band The Impact featured Rory. Arty and the other musicians were mesmerised by his playing of Chuck Berry standards and stayed around to watch. Just a few years later Rory was to draw on the resources of another showband by recruiting Richard McCracken and John Wilson who, some years earlier, had played alongside Derek Mehaffey in Derrick and the Sounds.

Tadgh Kidney, who was closely associated with the Crypt, remembers The Impact opening for Cat Stevens in 1965 in an Arcadia that was packed to the rafters. Cat Stevens had reached the charts that week with 'I Love My Dog'. Stevens told Rory and Donal that he was getting a little fed up of life on the road and was more interested in getting involved in production. He then went on to explain how the production process worked and his relationship with Paul Samwell Smith, formerly of The Yardbirds, in the recording studio. A few months later, Rory sat with Eric Burdon and The Animals in The Metropole Hotel hearing about life on the road and reaching the singles charts, something Rory had no interest in whatsoever, a disdain he held all through his career.

The Impact had to look outside Ireland for work and, in particular, to the German city of Hamburg where, in 1965, you could catch the Spencer Davis Group fronted by Stevie Winwood and Eric Burdon and the Animals. Rory again: 'Hamburg had a reputation of being second to Liverpool and London as, you know, the music centre. It was also like the museum of Rock and Roll because great albums were made there by Jerry Lee Lewis – *Live at the Star Club* – which I had at the time and still is one of the best live albums around. Gene Vincent and Fats Domino would bypass England and Ireland and do the Star Club – it was that important. So we didn't play the Star Club until later but we played a place called the Big Apple and we played in Lubech and it was just great to be there. It was kind of frightening when you saw Hamburg the first time, it was erm … it's just as well we didn't know how dangerous it was! It was a great starting ground. You were more or less allowed to play what you wanted. You had long sets to play – you'd play forty-five minutes of the hour for six sets a night, which wasn't that tough compared to some of the bands who used to have to do eight or nine sets and you'd get blisters on your left hand from that and sore throats but eh … Obviously when we got there, the Beatles had been and gone and a few of the other groups who became famous through Hamburg but the atmosphere was still there. This was '64/'65/'66 so we still got a flavour of the whole Beatles/Hamburg mystique and the clubs were still referring to "Oh we had the Beatles here recently and we had the Undertakers and the Searchers and The Big Three" – all these big groups. It was a fascinating place at the time.'

Detail of The Big Three EP, which inspired Rory's three-piece.

One of the more impressive gigs by The Impact was at the Pioneer and Total Abstinence Rallies which were held in the Savoy and Capitol cinemas. Distinguished broadcaster and film director Philip King remembers that, 'There was something about Rory's commitment to the music, and the abandon with which he played and his dedication to his craft. Rory was a maverick, in this country there was really not a lot of music on television, every thing was coming out of the radio, the showbands and what was then called popular music like Cliff Richard and The Beatles dominated the airwaves. The phenomenon of the group, the three-piece group, like Cream – they were known as the "Creams" in Cork – and Jimi Hendrix Experience, that sort of thing, Rory was our version of that and not alone was he as good as they were, there was something about the way he played which we could truly relate to. I think that "thing" was his sense of tradition. It might be a peculiar word to use in the context of a three piece rock band – you know, a guitar, bass, and drums – but Rory was a purist and a traditionalist at heart and his tradition was the country blues of America – Son House, Sonny Terry, Brownie McGhee, and Big Bill Broonzy – music he had heard through the songs of Lonnie Donegan when he was hardly in his teens and listening to American Forces Network coming out of the American military bases in Germany at the time. Also he was listening to Radio Luxembourg as we all were: his interpretation of that blues was shot through with his spirit of abandon and he declared how he was overpowered by the music and yet controlled and distilled it in his performances. The music was in many ways his mistress if you like and as it turned out at the end of his life, a very hard mistress and something he'd a very difficult relationship with. He mediated the music for me and all of us growing up here at the time.'

Rory left The Impact in early 1966 and began to sit in with local beat groups.

A Taste of Success

In Dayton, Ohio, on 31 July 1976 where Rory supported Aerosmith who were then riding high on the hit 'Walk This Way'. Rory captured their audience to the extent that they opened with their hit (to recapture the crowd) rather than closing their show with it (© Fin Costello).

ERIC KITTERINGHAM and Norman Damery, two friends of Rory Gallagher's, were the bass player and drummer with a Cork band called the Axills. The other members of the group were Derek 'Doc' Green, on vocals and lead guitar, and Peter Sanquest, on rhythm guitar and keyboards. The Axills were a clean-cut group who sang the hits of the day and modelled themselves quite openly on The Beatles. They split up in the summer of 1966 when Peter Sanquest left for London. Rory's group, The Impact, had just split up too. The three friends came together to form Taste. The decision was made, Eric recalled, over 'a glass of milk and a slice of chocolate at An Stad down by the Cavern Club'.

Pete Brennan, Eric's cousin and a member of the Lee Valley String Band for over thirty years, remembers Taste in their earliest days, when they were lugging equipment up to Eric's bedroom in his family home on Victoria Road. 'They were getting the equipment together and it was a case of "call everyone we know to lug the stuff up". The practice area was a large bedroom at the rear of the house and they were tinkering around up there. For some reason, the rest of us were chucked out as soon as they all started to play. That was my first meeting with Rory and we ended up that day out on the street playing football while the other lads were inside discussing tactics or whatever.'

Pete went to school at the Christian Brothers College near Rory's first home in Cork on MacCurtain Street – the family later moved to Sydney Park and then the suburb of Douglas. They'd often meet on the street or in Eason's or Ursula's Record Store. Rory's 'usual haunt', however, was still Crowley's, where he'd buy strings or just look at the equipment and instruments and books. Rory was eighteen by now and it was to the Pig and Whistle or Swan and Cygnet that he and his friends went to drink. Eric and Norman, who were both three years older than Rory, also had jobs at Guys Printing Works and Norwich Union respectively. Pete can remember Norman's family saying, 'It's very strange, Norman is working with an insurance company and getting involved in that long-haired music scene, those beat groups!'

The Retired Army Officers Club on MacCurtain Street was where Taste began proper rehearsals in 1966. The facilities and equipment were quite primitive and Pete Brennan was almost electrocuted trying to help out. 'There was a piece of electric cable, and I was supposed to be putting a plug on the other end of it. I was talking to somebody else. He got his end fixed before I did mine and we were both working putting a plug on either end of the one cable! He plugged his end in and I was still holding the live wire on the other end! That's the one thing I remember about the Army Club; I've burn marks on my fingers to prove it! The stupidity of what we used to do! That was at a Sunday afternoon practice.'

The Shandon Boat Club and the Cavern played host to Taste's first gigs during the late summer and autumn of 1966. They played every week if they could, or every second week, usually on Saturday nights. The Cavern was dingy and black, with a small staircase and an even smaller balcony. And yet the place was amazing, with an electric atmosphere. Unbelievably, John Mayall, the great English blues player, even performed there! The band and their friends would travel around, Pete Brennan recalls, in an old 'two-tone Bedford van with windows all around and a sliding door at the side that the lads used to rent for the Saturday night. Eventually, the lads bought an old Musgraves van, blue and white, and Eric hand-painted "Taste" onto the front of it. That van saw a lot of road!'

Early Taste Mark 1 handout featuring (l–r): Norman Damery, Rory and Eric Kitteringham (handout courtesy of Pete Brennan).

Led by Rory's playing, Taste soon had quite a reputation in Cork. What marked them out was the energy and primitive sound that Rory captured with his sparkling and astounding playing of the Stratocaster, especially on tracks like the Elmore James standard 'Dust My Blues', which Rory played bottle-neck style, or The Who's 'My Generation'. Another cover of the period they'd mastered was 'Heatwave', which began to appear regularly in the band's set list. 'With Taste, Rory never played songs in the same order,' said Eric. 'Normally a band would have a set program but you'd never know what Rory was going to churn out, ever, he'd just fire it out, and if there was a twenty-second break between numbers it was a lot. Get in, churn it out with high energy, go for it, break away from the very first note ... that was his style.'

The Taste back-line comprised of a 60-watt bass amplifier, a large speaker cabinet (almost 6 foot high with two 18-inch speakers in it and a tiny little Burns 60-watt double B amplifier on top of it), a Fender two by twelve cabinet and a Fender bass man piggy-back amp. Rory also had his VOX AC 30, which needed about three hours for the valves to warm up. Rory always placed the VOX AC 30 on a tubular steel chair. There had to be a chair: it was, according to Rory, the perfect height and when he went on to play major venues, he continued with this practice. He was always conscious that if the amp was placed on beer crates it was likely to fall, with the backrest on the chair he was assured of a safe passage. He blew all comers away with the sound he achieved from the VOX AC 30 – many other guitarists would plug in to a similar set up but could never come close to the sound he made.

Pete Brennan gave out Taste flyers at the early Cork gigs. 'You'd be torn apart if it was seen that you had them. If any woman saw them, you'd literally be savaged. If you had anything to do with the band, that was it, you were attractive to women, by association, if you were lucky, and you'd be surprised how many "hangers-on" there were with bands!' Rory, it had to said, cut quite a dash in Cork of the 1960s with his flowing long hair.

Pete also made an early tape recording, done on a Sanyo hand-held cassette player. 'Eric's brother Paddy Kitteringham and myself held it up and tried to record it, and you get more girls screaming

Facing page: These adverts, featuring Taste in various locations in June 1967, appeared in the *Evening Echo,* Cork's local paper.

than music, you can hear the thumping of a drum, you cannot hear any bass but you can definitely hear a lead guitar screaming all over the place, overshadowed by young women screaming and young fellows shouting. If you tried to release it as some sort of commercial recording, you could forget it, it's just mayhem, total mayhem!'

In 1967, the legendary DJ and publicist B. P. Fallon was one of the judges on an RTÉ radio show called *Spot the Talent*. The programme was broadcast live from the St Francis Xavier Hall in Dublin in front of an invited audience every Thursday night. It was an inter-county talent competition and, according to B. P., 'featured everything from W. B. Yeats recitations to ballad songs; there was even a juggler, all you could hear on the wireless was nervous coughing and the sound of the odd ball being dropped – riveting stuff.

'Come the week for Cork to field their team and, great gosh almighty, there among the three acts was a blues band. My co-adjudicators, they were appalled at this noisy trio, all guitar, bass and drums and seemingly very, very loud indeed. They played in a style loosely reminiscent of John Mayall's Bluesbreakers – and I loved them. So much so, in fact, that I gently informed my fellow judges that unless Cork, led by this blues trio, won this heat of *Spot the Talent* I, too, was out of the game. Thus the very first live radio broadcast by Taste, and a winner too.'

That same year saw Taste open for The Dubliners in the Savoy in their home town of Cork on Wednesday 7 June. They also opened for The Vards in the Arcadia, as well as continuing their regular Shandon Boat Club gigs. Elsewhere in the county, you could catch the Wolfe Tones in Midleton Golf Club; while *Mata Hari* was showing in The Ritz Cinema, starring Jeanne Moreau; *The Sound of Music* had opened in the Capitol Cinema; DJs Don (Rory's brother Donal) and Deen were playing the Cavern. Rory was to establish a lifelong contact with Ronnie Drew. They recorded 'Barley and Grape Rag' together and performed on stage at the Temple Bar Blues Festival in 1992. Ronnie also hosted a masterclass with Rory in the Guinness Hop Store as part of that festival.

UCCESS IN CORK was not enough for Rory. He was always talking with and learning from other bands, and realised in 1967 that Taste had to move to Belfast, which was an important spot for bands of the so-called 'British Blues Invasion'. 'The Beat scene was coming together and so we made the odd trips to Belfast and Dublin, Limerick, Waterford and Galway. You'd get enough work in a week to keep you ticking over. Bit by bit we started moving to Belfast as a jumping off place and we made the odd trip to the continent and to Hamburg.'

'The first night we played Belfast,' recalled Eric, 'we had no digs. We had nowhere to stay and I think it was around the time of the Ulster TT and all the guesthouses and bed-and-breakfasts were booked out. One of the lads in the other band said, if you're stuck come back to my place. We will give you the couch or the floor, there's no problem, it was Billy McCoy, and his mother put a full Ulster fry in front of us the following morning.' Eric loved Belfast, and will always have a soft spot for the city.

Eddie Kennedy became Taste's manager in Belfast. In August of 1966, he had travelled down from Belfast to the Cavern in Cork with his sixteen-year-old son Billy. He had come to see Taste, led by the most exciting guitarist in the country at the time. Kennedy, that fateful night in Cork, saw the raw power in young Rory Gallagher's playing.

Above and previous page: Taste – Norman Damery, Eric Kitteringham and a well-wrapped Rory at Bellevue in Belfast during the summer of 1967 on a break (courtesy of Frankie Griffin – a resolute Rory fan).

Rory created something really special on stage, bringing an aura to a room, no matter what its size. Kennedy was keen to take an up-and-coming act under his wing and bring them to a mass audience. It was a decision that has become part of our rock history. In the next four years that plan culminated with the DJ 'Kid' Jensen stating just a few weeks before their break-up after the legendary Isle of Wight festival in 1970 that 'I've just seen the band of the decade.'

Eddie Kennedy was from east Belfast. He and his wife, Maxi, were keen ballroom dancers and he started out booking ballroom dancing in the Maritime Hotel. Over time, he began booking other acts for the venue, which was the spiritual home and starting point for Van Morrison and Them. By 1968, Eddie had created Club Rado at the venue, the name inspired by a beach of the same name in Cannes in the south of France where he spent some time on holiday each year. Kennedy also promoted regular shows at the Floral Hall, the Ritz Cinema and the Ulster Hall in the city for bands, including the BeeGees, the Freshmen and the Miami Showband. Through his partnership with Robert Masters of NEMS booking agency, later to become the Robert Stigwood Organisation, he was central to finding support slots for Taste in Northern Ireland, opening for Cream, John Mayall and the Bluesbreakers, and Fleetwood Mac among others.

Eric Kitteringham remembered well the band's time with Fleetwood Mac. 'We did Belfast with them and Norman, at the time, had an Austin 1100 car and he decided he was going to drive up to Derry, so I headed up with him, and Rory travelled with the gear in the van. Kennedy said, "Would you take a couple of Mac with you in the car?" So Mick Fleetwood and Peter Green got into the car, and we headed off to Derry with the two of them in the back of the car, with Mick Fleetwood's legs touching the ceiling he was so tall. When we got to the Embassy in Derry, there was a massive queue outside the venue and the two lads took fright. "They look very mean," they said, so we reassured them. We walked down in the door, "How's it going?", they were great, they relaxed.'

Kennedy's connections also opened the door to gigs in London for Taste, at Blaises Club, the 100 Club, the Speakeasy and the Marquee. This last venue was particularly important and Eddie Kennedy's son, Billy, remembers that when visiting UK acts performed at Club Rado, they were introduced as 'Direct from London's Marquee' a badge of honour. Taste's first English gig, however, was actually as support for Captain Beefheart in the Britannia Rowing Club in Nottingham. Over the next year they toured the length of Britain in a converted Musgraves van which eventually packed up as they came down an exit ramp to a service station close to Watford Gap where they abandoned it.

Norman and Eric had given up their jobs in Cork by now and Taste were living in Belfast full-time and making regular visits to venues all over the UK. The relationship between Taste and Eddie Kennedy was close, with his wife, Maxi, looking after the three Cork boys, even darning their socks and sewing on shirt buttons. As a manager, Eddie also made sure they started getting a lot more money per gig than they had been in Cork.

Billy Kennedy remembers his father spending a considerable amount of time and effort promoting Taste and bringing them to a wider European audience. There was a spell in Germany when they met Cream, like Taste, they were a blues-influenced three-piece. 'The first time that I saw Cream,' recalled Eric, 'we had just finished our first stint at the Big Apple in Germany. We were due to come back, and then we discovered that Cream were playing in the Star Club in Hamburg on the same night, so instead of heading for the Hook of Holland to get the ferry, we went off into Hamburg: we were spellbound through the night. It was really amazing ... afterwards, we went to the stage door and said we were with the band, they stood back and opened the door, and we got chatting with them, they were lovely guys, that was a great experience.'

A less enjoyable experience arose out of a demo session the band recorded in July 1967 in Emerald Studios in Belfast, which was run by record distributor Mervyn Solomon. The tracks, mainly covers and never meant for release, were very raw and were to emerge on an album titled *In the Beginning* – issued on the Emerald/Gem label in 1974, when Rory was at the height of his fame. Rory was appalled, as he felt the album 'could have done untold damage'. It was finally withdrawn three years later following legal action.

Taste saw continued success in 1968. They had established a really strong reputation in the Marquee, Klooks Kleek, the Lyceum, the 100 Club and had shared the bill with Fleetwood Mac, Cream, and Jethro Tull throughout the UK. Rory was also developing as a performer and starting to write his own songs. It was a hard slog, though, on what were the early days of a touring circuit, with primitive roads, transport and equipment. They also had to survive on meagre rations, and Eric Kitteringham has the vivid memory of having to eat raw mushrooms when they were sharing a basement flat in Earls Court in London. The heavy touring was taking its toll. 'We would play Glasgow on a Sunday night,' Eric recalled, 'and be in the Marquee in London, Monday night. It was a long journey, it felt like 600 miles, and the roads were not what they are now. You only had motorway some of the way and Norman did most of the driving.'

In the summer of 1968, Taste played the Woburn Abbey Festival. Jimi Hendrix played the previous night to them. This was the beginning of the era of the open-air festival. The set-list included 'Baby Please Don't Go', 'Summertime', 'Blister on the Moon', 'You Shook Me Baby', and 'I Got My Brand On You'. Also on the bill were John Mayall and the Bluesbreakers, Tim Rose, one-man-band Duster Bennett, Family, Alexis Korner, Pentangle, Roy Harper, Shirley and Dolly Collins, and from New Orleans barrelhouse piano player Champion Jack Dupree. This was to be one of the final appearances by this Taste line-up in such stellar company.

The band returned to Belfast for a gig at Romano's Ballroom in August. It was the last time the original trio performed. Eddie Kennedy had decided to change the line-up, replacing Eric Kitteringham with Richard McCracken on bass guitar and Norman Damery with John Wilson on drums. Wilson and McCracken were young but experienced musicians. They were both from Belfast and had been playing most recently with an outfit called Cheese. Wilson had previously played drums with Them. Eddie Kennedy recognised their potential as sidemen alongside Rory Gallagher and so Norman and Eric, having

New Spotlight magazine headlines the return of Taste during the winter of 1969 with a four-page special spread.

done much of the slogging and groundwork, were replaced. Kennedy went on to establish contact with Roland Rennie, managing director of Polydor Records in London, and secured the new-look Taste a recording contract.

Rory's brother Donal had taken on the role of road manager from the summer of 1968. According to Eric, 'Donal came to see us and said Rory wants to see you upstairs. Rory broke the news then and said they were forming a different band.' Norman, who had just bought a brand new Ludwig drum kit, never played again.

John Wilson spoke to me recently about those years in Belfast. Eddie Kennedy, he believes, was well meaning. 'All bands, no matter what their size, need someone to take care of business and the day-to-day running of what a band does.' Of his time with Cheese, Wilson recalled how 'we couldn't get any gigs in Belfast because of the style of West Coast music that we played – we couldn't get arrested! Eddie Kennedy ran the Rado at The Maritime Hotel and liked our band. I'd meet Eddie on the street and he'd ask how the band was doing and he'd give you ten or twenty pounds to get yourself some food.' Kennedy got Cheese a few gigs in the Speakeasy in London. 'At the same time, Rory was coming up and down with Norman and Eric, and as musicians we all knew each other … I liked Rory a lot and I understood where he was at and what he was trying to say: that was obvious to me from the word go.'

His reaction to the departure of Eric and Norman, which he has never before spoken about publicly, was that 'Norman and Eric should be getting huge respect, huge respect, because they were the guys that got Rory to a place where he wanted to be. They were the two guys who played all the horrible gigs in pubs and clubs and slept on floors, mightn't get to eat for two days, travelled up and down from Cork to Belfast on a motorbike, ye'know, and they got no credit. No one ever mentions Norman and Eric … They were real nice guys but they didn't have any real musical experience to be able to rise to the occasion, neither did Rory at that time – Rory was still finding his way – but the point was from that Eddie Kennedy thing … Eddie Kennedy was the one who saw the potential in the very beginning. Eddie Kennedy was prepared to invest his time and money in Rory and Taste.'

Some iconic Taste album covers.

THE FIRST TIME I SAW RORY GALLAGHER PLAY was with the second line-up of Taste – John Wilson on drums and Richie McCracken on bass guitar – in the National Boxing Stadium on the South Circular Road in Dublin in 1968. I bumped into Rory in the gent's toilet, which was a fairly primitive affair in the Stadium, and like many young fans (I was sixteen) it was an amazing thing to meet your hero. As ever, Rory was the absolute gentleman and nodded and wished well to myself and my friend, Eddie Breslin. He said he looked forward to talking to us after the show. The Stadium in Dublin was the venue in the city at that time and, thanks to Jim Aiken, we got to see, throughout the course of the 1960s and 1970s, many of the top English bands including Led Zeppelin, Jethro Tull, Fleetwood Mac, John Mayall's Bluesbreakers and The Nice.

Wilson and McCracken started out, like Rory, with a showband, with Derek Mehaffey of Derrick and the Sounds. They then had a band called Cheese. Wilson, the more extroverted of the two, was a very strong drummer, and McCracken, an accomplished bass player. Over the coming two years, this power trio would conquer audiences all over Europe, from Belfast, Dublin, and Cork, to the Marquee in London and the Star Club in Hamburg which was made world-famous by The Beatles. Wilson felt that when he and McCracken 'came aboard the group was certainly elevated to new heights and often Rory and ourselves were transported to great heights by the energy of the playing and the intensity'.

Taste established a major following and took up the mantle left by Cream and the Jimi Hendrix Experience. 'Bit by bit, after we moved to Belfast, we started to make a strong foothold in London, thanks mainly to the Marquee Club and a few other places like that,' Rory recalled. 'This sounds like it happened in six months – it didn't. We

Words – the iconic song lyric publication, which mirrored the pop charts, with Rory Gallagher on the cover.

got a record contract and we started working on the first album, but at this point we'd done nearly every club up and down the country and quite a few festivals on the continent, so we cut the first album in late '68, it was released in early 1969.

'At this stage I'd written quite a few songs myself and I was trying to develop my own style so to speak, but you'd still be ultra aware of all the greats, I mean, and you'd be trying to get this album and that album and check back to what they did and try to keep up to date with what they were playing. I mean, if you're a rock and roll or blues traditionalist by nature, you still try and … you still look up to these people as opposed to people of the same age as yourself and so on. So you just try and follow what they're doing at that particular time and, at the same time, you're well aware there's no point in just being a copyist, being over-influenced by this artist or that. You're just trying to develop your own guitar and vocal style and write, you know, new ideas.'

The band's first studio album *Taste* captured something of the essence of their energy live and was released in 1969 with standout tracks 'Blister on the Moon' and 'Born on the Wrong Side of Time' composed by Rory Gallagher. Taste were hailed by the music press and the growing public following as the next big thing. The album sold over two hundred thousand copies worldwide within a year of its release and is still selling today. The following year saw the release of *On the Boards*, which charted the progress this power house trio had made on the road. John Wilson: 'In the early days the big thing was John Peel's late night radio show. Everybody listened to it and I can remember vividly travelling over the Pennines and waiting eagerly to hear the first play of our first single "Blister on the Moon".'

Rory and the second Taste line-up were to perform in 1968 at Cream's farewell concert in the Royal Albert Hall, part of a stellar bill playing homage to Jack Bruce, Ginger Baker, and Eric Clapton. A few months later, Taste were invited to join the newly-formed Blind Faith – the supergroup to emerge out of the ashes of Cream – on a tour of the US and Canada.

Blind Faith featured Ginger Baker on drums, Eric Clapton on guitar and vocals, Stevie Winwood from a temporarily disbanded Traffic on keyboards, guitar, and vocals, and Rick Grech from Family on bass, violin, and vocals. Blind Faith were, for the time, unique. They were dubbed the prototype 'supergroup' where the interest focussed on the performers rather than the unit. They recorded Buddy Holly's 'Well All Right' coupled with a Winwood original 'Can't Find My Way Home'. The album also included 'Had to Cry Today' and 'Sea of Joy' by Stevie Winwood, 'Presence of the Lord' by Eric Clapton and closed with Ginger Baker's 'Do What You Like'. Their debut album achieved more notoriety for its cover photo of a thirteen-year-old girl than for its content and, within a few months, they had disbanded. Clapton went on to form the more low-key Derek and the Dominoes, Ginger Baker went off to form Airforce, Winwood and Grech rejoined a revamped Traffic and later went to work with the 'Grievous Angel' Gram Parsons.

Rory on the Blind Faith tour: 'We got an opening to play on the show and that was our first trip to the States, about six weeks, the other support was Delaney and Bonnie and Friends, and the people in that band were ridiculous – you had Leon Russell, J. J. Cale would be there, and Jim Gordon and all these famous players so you'd learn just standing side stage watching these people.'

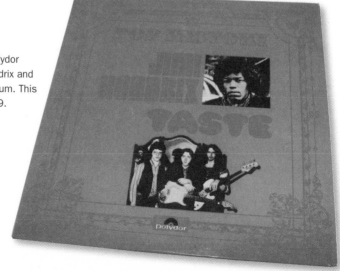

Vinyl of pairing by Polydor Germany of Jimi Hendrix and Taste in a double album. This was released in 1969.

Delaney Bramlett met Bonnie Lynn in 1967 and legend has it that within five days they'd married. Delaney was one half of the Shindogs – a duo – with his partner Joey Cooper. They were resident on Jack Good's US TV show *Shindig*. Bonnie had been playing with Fontella Bass and Albert King before she became a member of the Ikettes alongside Ike and Tina Turner. Their Friends outfit was made up of Leon Russell, Jerry McGee (ex-Ventures guitarist), Bobby Whitlock, Carl Radle, Jim Keltner, Bobby Keyes, Jim Price, and Rita Coolidge. They were to make up the blueprint for what became Mad Dogs and Englishmen the following year alongside Joe Cocker.

Rory's first tour stateside was on this caravanserai and, according to Donal, 'He'd never seen crowds quite like it, a lot of fans went berserk and there was a fair bit of activity from bouncers and police beating people up and things: it was very scary. The first gig was in Philadelphia, at the Spectrum, on a revolving stage, so it was going around Beatles-fashion and between that and having our first experience of jet lag, I tell you it was serious. Taste went down well and later we went on to Baltimore and Boston and we played an open air gig in Boston, and Janis Joplin showed up at the gig in Boston. Given that this was Rory's first time in America, everything was quite different to Europe – things like all-night television, all-night food and the availability of certain instruments and records. It was quite good, but as usual, it was so hectic, you couldn't really absorb anything.'

John Wilson knew that 'Rory never liked playing large venues, and was not very fond of major stadium gigs and ice hockey arenas that we encountered on the Blind Faith tour of the USA and Canada.' Proximity to a supergroup certainly left Rory with mixed feelings. He spoke to Charles Fisher of the *London Evening Standard*: 'We don't put any gimmicks into it to make Taste a supergroup. We'd hate to just play three concerts a year here because we're basically the sweaty two pound ten a night group. So far we've stayed nice and naïve and pretty raw. Once you lose the essence of that, you're in a difficult position. What knocks me out the most is getting on a stage, playing a song and the people like it and are with you – as compared to sitting at home reading glossy magazines with massive super-group type write ups.

'We're wrapped up in taking, as far as possible, the three-piece, that tight little group and doing what you can with it as compared to getting pre-recorded tapes, and augmenting string quartets, or augmenting symphony orchestras. That's all right for some bands, but we're in that small band or outfit, keeping close to our roots, the blues.

'In my lyrics, I don't put across politics. I just put emotions or feelings. I don't use my lyrics as a weapon, you know, "Kick Heath" or "put someone else in" or whatever. I'm rarely knocked out by that sort of song because they are just newspaper headlines most of the time. I find my lyrics important for putting over the feeling or atmosphere.'

On the surface, things just seemed to get better for Taste the following year – 1970. That summer they appeared at the Isle of Wight festival on the Friday night in the company of Procul Harum, Arrival, Melanie, Family, Cactus, and The Voices of East Harlem. The following two days saw appearances by Ten Years After, The Who, Sly and the Family Stone, Miles Davis, Free, Mungo Jerry, John Sebastian, The Doors, Emerson, Lake and Palmer, Ralph McTell, Tiny Tim, Richie Havens, The Moody Blues, Jethro Tull, Pentangle, Jimi Hendrix, Joan Baez, and Leonard Cohen. On the Wednesday and Thursday, music fans had already seen Tony Joe White, Supertramp, Kris Kristofferson, Black Widow, and The Groundhogs ... a who's who of 1970s rock.

But if the Isle of Wight appearance, later released as a live album, was the zenith of Taste's success, it also marked the beginning of the end for the band. Within a few months, this three-piece, the natural inheritors of the Cream mantle, had split up, and at the end the three musicians were hardly on speaking terms

7

On The Boards

The second line up of Taste, photographed by Roy Esmonde in Earls Court, London, in June 1970, for a session for *Spotlight Magazine*: (l–r): Richard McCracken (bass guitar), John Wilson (drums) and Rory (lead guitar/vocals) (© Roy Esmonde).

ON THE BOARDS, Taste's second studio album, was a landmark for Rory Gallagher, who composed all the tracks from the opening spine-tingler 'What's Going On' – a short burst of high energy coming in at under three minutes – to the freeform jazz of the title track 'On the Boards'. The credits are very sparse on the liner notes with the producer credits going to Tony Colton by arrangement with Eddie Kennedy. Tony Colton was one of the founder members of England's greatest country band, Heads Hands and Feet, just a few years later, with Albert Lee on guitar. The planned sleeve notes were to have been written by Pat Egan as he mentioned in his end of year column in 1969 that Eddie Kennedy had invited him to compile them.

The second track on the album, like all of this repertoire, was never performed again by Rory following Taste's demise in December 1970. 'Railway and Gun' highlights the strength of the Cork musician's dexterity which had matured on and off stage over the previous few years developing into a good old fashioned twelve bar blues. On 'It's Happened Before, It'll Happen Again', Rory doffs his cap to his not widely known interest in jazz and the work of Charlie Christian and Wes Montgomery. This track stands out for Rory's exquisite scat singing and his counterpoint to Wilson and McCracken on drums and bass and represents the epitome of their increasingly jazz-led repertoire.

The album moves to a reflective blues, pondering the passage of time in 'If the Day Was Any Longer' and a fine harmonica solo from Rory who, at this stage, had also mastered banjo, mandolin, and saxophone. While his playing of the banjo and saxophone disappeared with the end of Taste, he continued to feature the blues harp or harmonica. 'Morning Sun' has that coarser edge to the Stratocaster with Rory constantly changing the tone and the pace to a walking blues and an ode to the elusive beauty of nature.

In an homage to his slide guitar heroes Earl Hooker and Elmore James, Rory opens 'Eat My Words' with some delicious slide playing on his Fender Telecaster, taking complex solos against John and Ritchie. On this outing, his scat singing style returns to imitate the guitar line.

The title track, 'On the Boards' is reflective and a paean to the solitary nature of music and of life itself. It is freeform in style and highlights, in particular, the understanding between each member of the trio. As John Wilson remembers, 'on certain nights on stage the band reached great creative heights and were transported'. This track also stands out because of Rory's superlative sax playing, and dominates the album as the longest track at just over six minutes.

Using echo on his vocal and opening with a sax line and transferring to harmonica, 'If I Don't Sing I'll Cry' was a firm 'live' favourite with a chopping guitar style perfected by Rory. 'See Here' is similar in style to a composition from some years later, 'I'm Not Awake Yet'. It is the odd man out on the album and yet has hints of his later writing ... Rory questioning his ability to master something. In effect, it's a workout on guitar showcasing his talent.

With a thunderous finish and another stage favourite of the time 'I'll Remember' closes out the album with vigorous harmonics in Rory's vocal and guitar playing – of all the tracks on the album it gives a clue as to what was to come with his solo outfit following the break up of Taste.

Jackie Hayden, formerly the general manager of *Hot Press* and now a contributing editor, worked with Polydor Records in Dublin during Taste's days on the label. 'I'd got involved with Polydor because I was working for Siemens, the German domestic appliance company. I had the job of pricing invoices by hand, which is something that people today might not fully understand and they [Siemens] had a small record department that was primarily Deutsche Grammophon classical records. But they had also started Polydor as a sort of easy listening James Last type label and then, lo and behold, they started having pop hits with people like the BeeGees and this kind of freaked the reserved Siemens staff out and they had no idea how to deal with this. And somehow I heard of a vacancy in the department, applied, and I think they were glad to get rid of me out of the invoice pricing game into the music. That's literally how I came to spend the rest of my life in the music business.'

Jackie remembers seeing Taste in a club in Mary Street in Dublin. 'It might have been called Club A Go Go, I'm not sure. It was an extraordinary experience because you went to gigs, you saw ballad groups perform or you saw a pop group playing in a tennis hop or whatever, but to see a guy up on stage – I remember I was very close to the front of the stage – putting such power and energy and sweating, pop stars didn't sweat, showband people didn't sweat … this guy was just working his ass off, and it was so exhilarating. It was an extraordinary experience and I was hooked from that point on.

'I remember being at Polydor when *On the Boards* came out, in fact, I have an autographed copy of the album signed by the three guys, and around that time Rory used to come over to Polydor's office sometimes and we'd plan some sort of publicity campaigns on a fairly innocent level. Neither Rory nor the industry of the time were geared for any high powered marketing strategies and, in fact, Rory really felt uncomfortable sometimes with these kinds of discussions.

'With Polydor located in Baggot Street, I remember Rory used to prefer if we went down to O'Donoghues Pub on Merrion Row just to have a chat to tease out a few things. He wasn't really comfortable being in an office with people, with the "suits" as it were, talking and using words like strategy, marketing or product.

'Territories was another one that he wouldn't have liked at all! We'd go down to O'Donoghues (where the legendary Luke Kelly and the Dubliners formed) and we'd have maybe a pint or an Irish coffee and chat about setting up a few interviews and maybe trying to get a few more radio plays. Given that we had one radio station at the time, Radio Éireann [now RTÉ Radio 1], it wasn't very easy.

'Radio Éireann was geared for playing music that was either very safe and or Irish, like Dermot O'Brien's accordion band (The Turfman from Ardee), Count John McCormack or very old ballads ranging to easy listening material such as Burl Ives or stuff like the Ray Conniff Singers. We had no problem having them played on the radio but any real serious rock music was virtually impossible, particularly since Rory wasn't into having hit singles!

'That didn't help either, so you tried to promote his records through record shops, people in shops who were tuned into rock music, maybe people in clubs, the odd DJ might feature a track here or there. Something like "Blister on the Moon" was a great track, even now it's a great track in a club or anywhere, it has remarkable power. So you tried to kind of find ways of promoting the stuff, making people more aware of it and, in fairness to Rory, he was always cooperative and eager to do things once he felt you were doing it for the music and not just doing it to shift "units of product".'

8
Taste Split

The *Melody Maker* edition of 12 September 1970 announces that 'Taste Fight Split'.
The group was no more by the end of the year.

Melody Maker

Zeppelin special — TURN TO PAGE 16

SEPTEMBER 12, 1970 1s weekly USA 25 cents

TASTE FIGHT SPLIT

TASTE narrowly averted a split last between themselves threatened to wreck the group.

A spokesman for Polydor, their record company, said: "It was over a question of general policy — definitely not musical policy — which has been coming to a head for some time.

"They've been stalling over it for quite a long time, but they had it out between themselves at the weekend. It's all sorted out now, and there's no question of them splitting up."

After their triumphant appearance at the Isle of Wight Festival, Taste appear to be on the verge of a major breakthrough, and are currently on a British concert tour.

The MM was tipped off about the possibility of a split by three anonymous telephone calls this week. Rumours of trouble were flying around backstage at the Fairfield Halls, Croydon, last Sunday, the opening night of the group's Polydor-promoted tour with Stone The Crows and Jake Holmes.

There were also reported to be "several complications" regarding the taping of their second appearance on BBC-2's Disco 2 show.

The BBC were apparently under the impression that the group had split, and set about finding a replacement for the show.

● SEE PAGE 20 for a review of the opening night of Taste's British tour.

Sebastian in free concert

JOHN SEBASTIAN will top the bill at Saturday's free concert in London's Hyde Park.

...so on the bill for the concert, which ...take place at the same venue as the ...one in July, will be ...d Heat and Eric ...n and War

...ned Heat will be ...g despite the death ...er guitarist Alan ...last week. He will ...placed by guitarist ...cott Hill, who has ...sly played with ...Heat in America ...pleting the line-up ...Ground, an Ameri-...oup, the Michael ... Band.

RORY GALLAGHER of Taste in action

Pink Floyd ballet!

Joe Cocker story

FULL STORY: STARTS ON

Jazzman's dilemma

SPECIAL ON

'**T**ASTE FIGHT SPLIT' declared the cover of *Melody Maker* on Thursday 12 September 1970, with a classic full-page photo of Rory, eyes closed, checked shirt and the Telecaster with the capo near the machine head of the guitar. 'Taste narrowly averted a split last week when disagreements between themselves threatened to wreck the group. A spokesman for Polydor, their record company, said "It was over a question of general policy – definitely not musical policy – which has been coming to a head for some time. They've been stalling over it for quite a long time, but they had it out between themselves at the weekend. It's all sorted out now; there is no question of them splitting up."

'After their triumphant appearance at the Isle of Wight Festival, Taste appear to be on the verge of a major breakthrough, and are currently on a British concert tour. The *Melody Maker* was tipped off about the possibility of a split by three anonymous telephone calls this week. Rumours of trouble were flying around backstage at the Fairfield Halls, Croydon, last Sunday, the opening night of the group's Polydor-promoted tour with Stone the Crows and Jake Holmes. There were also reported to be "several complications" regarding the taping of their second appearance on BBC 2's *Disco 2* TV show. The BBC were apparently under the impression that the group had split, and set about finding a replacement.'

A review of the opening night of the Taste tour appeared inside the issue. The writer, Roy Hollingworth, focused on Taste, Free, The Moody Blues, and Ten Years After with the question 'Is fan worship coming back?'

'At the Isle of Wight, Taste played a pretty normal set of music. They were, truthfully, nothing outstanding, and yet a whole field of people went totally wild. This type of fervour has followed Taste across the towns and cities of this country, and abroad. I remember seeing them at Buxton, where a host of excellent bands, including the Strawbs and Matthews Southern Comfort, played delightful sets, oozing with beautiful music, but failed miserably with the audience.'

With Taste, however, 'the music was good, but not exceptional, yet there and then we had hysteria'.

'Clive Woods of Polydor Records – Taste's label – says "I'm quite serious when I say this. When you go to a Taste concert, it's just like going to church. I've never seen such worship, such a religious following for a band. I don't think any of the others can really be

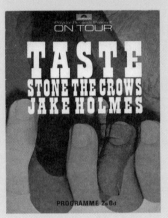

Taste's 'What's Going On' (shown here as the 7-inch single in a colour sleeve, 45 rpm) was played by the legendary DJ John Peel in 1969 – he loved it so much he played it three times in a row on the first hearing. Peel, who was hugely supportive of the band, had given the first airplay to Taste's debut single 'Blister on the Moon', which was released on the Major Minor label the previous year. The band heard it being played as they drove over the Pennines in the north of England.

Taste toured with Scotland's Stone the Crows and singer-songwriter Jake Holmes close to the band's eventual break-up in December 1970.

compared. I mean, when I have been at Taste concerts, I have seen Rory Gallagher stop playing, and the audience will get up in the silence, and it's a strange feeling but you can still hear him playing – through them. It's fantastic; complete hysteria. When Taste go, they go like a train, and they take everyone with them. There is silence as they play, this almost reverent hush, and they go wild at the end. They are very close to their audience; it's not a claustrophobic feeling, it's more togetherness. Taste have worked damned hard for this though, damned hard. Their last long player [LP] sold well, and I am confident that their next will sell millions."'

Hollingworth continues, 'Taste guitarist, Rory Gallagher, could not explain why this was happening, and preferred to look at it in a basic light. "I don't think it has become religious, but I agree there seems to be something more than music in it. But with us I don't think they are digging a big social thing. We try and avoid addressing our audience with something unnatural. We just go out and play. If they want to leap and freak about, and do strange things during the act, then that's okay with us," said Rory.'

But this fan worship was not enough to keep the band together. A few weeks later, in the 17 October issue of *Melody Maker*, the same writer was chronicling the demise of Taste. 'How Taste managed to stick together over the last month can only be described as a miracle. There was a massive sense of uneasiness during the whole Polydor tour of Britain with labelmates Stone the Crows (fronted by Maggie Bell). Rory Gallagher was almost in solitary confinement, and he joined Richie McCracken and John Wilson only when the group took to the stage.'

'It wasn't a case of us not speaking to him,' John Wilson told Hollingworth, 'he just didn't want to know us. He wouldn't travel with us in the group bus – he'd be in the van, he'd walk away from us: that's no way for a group to exist. We worked with him on stage, of course, because we were musicians, and part of a group – but it must be general knowledge that we've been playing crap for the last year.' This latter claim would be much disputed by fans at the time.

Wilson also told Hollingworth that he didn't like talking about Rory in such terms, 'but I've got to be honest about the way things were going, because when he spoke to the press, he made things out to be rosy. He really made us feel that he was the superstar, this was terrible. Sometimes he'd really muck us up – sometimes treating us on stage as though we never existed. I mean, it just began to go too far when he'd do three solo numbers on the run, other times he'd start off a 12 bar and then suddenly play on 9 bars, really trying to mess us up.'

After the break-up, £35,000 worth of bookings had to be cancelled. Eddie Kennedy, 'whose brilliant managership', according to Hollingworth, had 'taken Taste from a few quid a night in Cork to a steady £2,000 a gig is extremely upset about the break.' Kennedy: 'I've devoted two and a half years to putting them where they are now, and then this thing happens. Gallagher could have been a dollar millionaire by next year, and John and Richie wouldn't have been too badly off either. Rory was being paid more than the other two given the scale of his contribution, the other two were willing to accept this up to a point, but when they found out that Rory thought he was employing them, well, who's to say who is right, I'm not going to.'

A few weeks on from the Taste break-up, Rory stated simply, 'I don't want to get wound up about this. I don't hold grudges and some of the

Gallagher: I don't believe in public squabbles

'John Wilson, Richie McCracken and I were at a complete end not only musically but also as a group of people,' said Rory Gallagher about the break with his mates in Taste.

At the time of the split, Rory was praised for keeping his cool and not making statements about what had gone wrong . . . 'I don't believe in public squabbling between members of bands so I had no intention of knocking anyone,' he said last week. 'That saga that's going on between John Lennon and Paul McCartney is the greatest ever waste of space. Just think of all the young bands who could benefit from the columns taken up with their nonsense.'

Rory told me he was very glad that John and Ritchie had found the kind of band to suit their style . . . 'I have heard them only on disc so I could not make a judgement,' he said.

After only six weeks on Release, Rory's album Deuce has sold about 17,000 copies . . . That's about a thousand more than the first one.

Rory did not agree with my contention that the first set was better and that the releases should have been reversed . . . 'I was looking for a raw earthy sound on Deuce and I was fairly pleased with it,' he said. How about the lack of chart success with the two albums? — 'Well, Deuce made the top twenty for one week, I guess I was a little disappointed but not depressed. After all 17,000 albums is not bad.'

Will the next Gallagher album be a live one? — 'If we can find a suitable venue we will definitely do a live recording though it may not be the next release.'

If Rory hadn't formed Taste and found eventual success in Britain, would he have come back and joined a showband? — 'No, definitely not. I might have been into something else but never a showband.

How did he feel about bands such as the Royal and Dixies splitting yet finding new strength? — 'It's amazing. Some of them must have the secret of eternal youth.

In going to troubled Belfast to do a show was he seeking some kind of hero tag? — 'I didn't regard it as anything more than another gig. It's music I'm into and as long as there are people to listen I'll be there to play to them. You must be joking when you mention that hero bit.'

PAT EGAN

In this edition of *Bananas*, a *Spotlight* magazine special supplement, Rory explained, for the first time in print, the Taste split and how life on the road goes on, telling Pat Egan, 'I don't believe in public squabbles.'

people involved were out of their depth. Contrary to what appeared in print, I never made a penny out of Taste. The whole thing made me very wary of music business people. I don't give a damn about the money; it's people who let you down that bothers me the most.' A year later, in late 1971, Rory had the following to say to Pat Egan in *New Spotlight*: 'John Wilson, Richie McCracken and I were at a complete end, not only musically but also as a group of people ... I don't believe in public squabbling between members of bands so I had no intention of knocking anyone. That saga that's going on between John Lennon and Paul McCartney is the greatest ever waste of space: just think of all the young bands who could benefit from the columns taken up with their nonsense.'

The simple truth is that we may never know the full story behind the break-up, and Rory was always reluctant to revisit or speak about the period.

The next time John Wilson was to meet up with Rory was in the mid-1970s at a meeting of the Northern Ireland Guitar Society in Belfast, of which Rory was the patron. It was a happy reunion, where time had, indeed, healed old wounds. I spoke to Wilson recently about the final few months of Taste and his time with Rory in general: 'There was never a moment during those touring days of Rory, myself and Richie ever sitting down and discussing our future or business or what money was coming in; we left all that to Eddie Kennedy and trusted him to take care of that detail. The night before we played the Isle of Wight Festival, we'd been playing at the Lyceum in the Strand and when we came back to Earls Court our gear was still in the van, that night the van was burgled and everything, with the exception of Rory's VOX AC 30, was taken, so we had to beg and borrow to cobble together gear for the performance at the festival. It did not affect our playing but certainly the mood within the band had changed for the worse and from then out there was little chance of recovery. About four or five months earlier I'd purchased a little Ludwig drum kit, I'd hardly used it more than twice and that night I'd used the kit. I'd bought the kit from Vic O'Brien's shop in London, the kit was very personal and precious to me. That particular night, it was stolen along with all my cymbals, snare drum … the whole Isle of Wight was extremely difficult but it did not get in the way of the performance. Of course, the next weekend *Melody Maker* had "Taste Split" all over the front cover.

'Rory felt that he was being pushed in the wrong direction, more towards *Top of the Pops* and this was not a place he wanted to go. It would have been soul destroying for Rory,' said Wilson. 'Because of our attitude, we were anti-establishment, no riders on contracts, no frills. It didn't matter if there were two people or two thousand in the audience, we did the show and gave it our all.

'Some of the best gigs I did with Rory were in front of small crowds like the Argus Butterfly Workingmens' Club in Sunderland or the YMCA in Kirkcaldy: those were some of the best times, us just playing music – that was what we did best. You have to remember myself and Richie were seasoned musos – Rory didn't drink or anything, then occasionally he'd have a beer and he was great fun to be with. I've no particular memories about the Cream farewell gig or the Isle of Wight; it's the more intimate shows that hold the sweetest memories. Getting those instruments out of their cases and playing as if your life depended on it. It's all about the playing, my role in the band as the drummer was to make all the other members of the band sound better and tighter than they are.'

John Wilson was born a year before Rory in 1947 and feels that that grey area of the split business remains something of a mystery to this day. 'Rory had allegedly gone to manager Eddie Kennedy with a number of questions as to monies coming in, although even today that seems unlikely, knowing Rory. The scenario appeared to be that Rory was running the band, that it was his gig and that me and Richie were to be on a wage, but we were never told! We joined the band as a three piece band and Richie and I were well established as musicians and … somebody somewhere had sown these seeds of discontent. When I went to Eddie Kennedy at the time, he said, "Rory said he wanted you to be on a wage". I couldn't believe Rory saying that and all I was told was that the money was invested. A year later, when my wife and I set out to buy a house the bank manager was able to tell me that there was no money left … he even went so far as to offer me a drink before he delivered the news.

'None of us saw any of the money. We got an envelope each week to cover expenses and food and it all came to a stop after that final gig in Queen's University in Belfast. I'd been a musician since I was fifteen, so, along with guitarist Jim Cregan, we went off and did what we do – play music and formed Stud. There was no way we could re-create what we did with Taste and with Rory – he was one of the "special ones" and it would have been quite some-thing to find another. I genuinely feel and so, I believe, did Rory, that if the business had been handled in a different manner then it may never have led to the break-up of something so special.'

The top Irish albums in the *Banana* supplement, dominated by Rory.

Rory, with his brother and manager Donal, heads for the stage in Dayton, Ohio, in 1976. He shared the bill with Aerosmith and The Rick Derringer Band (© Fin Costello).

9

Going It Alone

THE FIRST RORY GALLAGHER solo album was released in 1971. *Rory Gallagher* – or the black album as we'll call it – still showed signs of Gallagher's direction with Taste. His line-up of musicians also drew on Belfast again, with Gerry McAvoy on bass guitar and Wilgar Campbell on drums and percussion. Rory featured on vocals, guitar, alto saxophone, mandolin and harmonica.

Wilgar Campbell came from the beat scene in Belfast, having played in, The Method in 1968 alongside Paul Hanna on bass guitar and the incredibly talented guitarist Dave Lewis, who was to go on and form Andwellas Dream who signed to CBS Records. Wilgar left The Method to join Deep Joy and played behind Jim Ferguson on lead guitar and a young Gerry McAvoy on bass guitar. Deep Joy supported Taste in 1969 on some of their Irish tour dates. Wilgar Campbell had replaced Brendan O'Neill on drums with Deep Joy; in a few years' time, Brendan was to join Rory's band alongside McAvoy.

Deep Joy played their final gig in the Ulster Hall on New Year's Eve 1970. A few weeks later, early in the New Year, Rory called bass player Gerry McAvoy to a rehearsal room in London. Also trying out for the new outfit at the time were former Hendrix sticks man Mitch Mitchell and bassist Noel Redding as well as bassist Rob Strong (father of *The Commitments* star Andrew). Gerry McAvoy and Wilgar were to be the other members of the Rory Gallagher Band, and with Rory signing to Polydor, his business affairs were taken in harness by David Oddie. Oddie later went on to form the Quarry Agency with his other major act, Status Quo.

Armed with his trusty Fender Telecaster, Rory gives his usual thumbs up at the close of an energetic set in Queen Elizabeth Hall, London, September 1971 (courtesy John Crone).

Rory on stage of the Queen Elizabeth Hall, London, September 1971. In the photograph on the left, Rory is playing his Stratocaster; on the right, he has his Telecaster (both courtesy John Crone).

Rory continued to base himself in Philbeach Gardens in Earls Court. The debut solo album was recorded in Advision Studios in London. It was produced by Rory and engineered by Eddie Offord, who had handled desk duties on *On the Boards*. This black-sleeved album features a smiling Rory on the cover by photographer Mick Rock, who was working with the design studio Hipgnosis at the time. Hipgnosis were the leading sleeve designers, led by artist Storm Thorgeson and Roger Dean – if it had a strong sleeve and was on vinyl then Hipgnosis was the team involved. They had designed covers for Pink Floyd, Led

53

Zeppelin, 10CC, YES, Peter Gabriel, UFO, Argent, and Wings. Take a look at the cover for Argent's *In Deep* and see where Nirvana, several decades later, received their inspiration for *Nevermind*.

This was a new, re-charged Gallagher, with any record collection being assembled in Ireland in 1971 having the two black albums as their bedrock – *Planxty* and *Rory Gallagher*.

The album opened with what was to become a classic 'Gallagher' guitar riff. It was inspired by the public 'Laundromat' located in the basement of his Earls Court flat. This was followed by 'Just a Smile', an acoustic outing acknowledging the English folk boom and the legacy of such wonderful players as Davy Graham, Richard Thompson, Bert Jansch, with whom he was later to record.

Rory's two stand-out tracks on this album are 'Hands Up' and 'Sinner Boy', which became constants in his set list over the next three decades. They are both reflective of the missed opportunities that the demise of Taste presented but also the musical horizons that beckoned. It is remarkable to consider that Gallagher was capable of writing this material at twenty-three given the upheaval that the break-up had caused, both professionally and personally. The turmoil that resulted from this split reverberated until his passing and he was never comfortable speaking about this period in his career.

'Wave Myself Goodbye', another acoustic tour de force, features the New Orleans bar-room style piano accompaniment provided by Vincent Crane of Atomic Rooster, with whom Rory's brother Donal had been acting as tour manager following the demise of Taste. It's almost a talking blues and relaxed in style and execution.

'It's You', while country in style, is a reference to the skiffle beginnings and a unique pedal steel slide and the double tracked mandolin which is somewhat lost in the mix. The mandolin was later to become a fixture in the live show and featured in 'Going to My Home Town'.

The original vinyl album (available today on CD and remastered vinyl) featured a jazz-oriented workout, seeking solace as ever and waiting for time to stand still in 'Can't Believe It's True' with Rory featuring on saxophone, an instrument he was to feature occasionally in the band line-up with 'Irish' John Earle.

Perhaps the most moving and reflective composition on the black album is the introspective 'I Fall Apart', which today still moves many

Tour advertisement for the 1970s, note particularily the two nights in a row in Liverpool and then the show in Manchester: the north of England held a huge fan base for the Cork guitarist.

of his more mature fans to tears with his lyrical guitar playing where he makes the notes cry on the Stratocaster.

Also recorded for these sessions but omitted from the original vinyl release were two blues gems – 'Gypsy Woman' penned by his teenage idol Muddy Waters with whom he was to record the following year for the *London Sessions* on Chess Records, and 'It Takes Time', composed by Chicago blues guitar titan Otis Rush. Both are included on the CD reissue of this album as bonus tracks.

The album took only three weeks to record and was warmly received. Nevertheless, it was outside the studio environment and it was in a live concert setting that the real heart and soul of Rory's solo work was to be heard, defined a few years later by both *Live in Europe* and *Irish Tour 74*. 'We never end a show on a low note,' said Rory around this time. 'In any one set, we do a couple of slow blues, a couple of straight ahead rockers, a few songs that are in between somewhere and we try to end the night on a good high feeling. It's very difficult and fractured to get too analytical about what you play or perform because every gig is different: we don't even use a set list; we change the set every night.'

Rory's self-titled debut album was followed the next year by *Deuce*. This time the tracks were laid down in Tangerine Studios, which had been started by the legendary Joe Meek next to a bingo hall in Dalston in north London. The same musicians were involved, with Rory on vocals, guitar, and mandolin, Gerry McAvoy on bass, and Wilgar Campbell on drums. However, this time around, as in many successive outings, the intention was to capture the 'live' feel. All compositions on this album were written by Rory. The album opened with a paean to life on the road, that of a troubadour or vaudevillian as Rory saw it, 'I'm Not Awake Yet', waiting for that knock on the hotel room door. He was to perform this in an acoustic setting in his final performance on

Rory signs another autograph for an ardent fan
backstage (© Fin Costello).

Irish soil in 1993 as the headline act at the Cork Regional Technical College in their inaugural arts festival.

'In Your Town' builds up right from the off and you can hear where Philip Lynott and Thin Lizzy found their inspiration for 'Jailbreak'. Rory takes on the crowd with strong slide playing á la Earl Hooker and Tampa Red and duelling or cutting contests with his sidemen on bass and drums. 'There's a Light' is almost a farewell to his jazz influences and his interest in Charlie Christian that was such an integral part of the overall Taste sound and that freeform playing and loose format. This is followed by a classic twelve bar blues 'Should've Learnt my Lesson' in the tradition of Chicago blues at the Checkerboard Lounge or the Macomba Lounge, revisiting the sound of his heroes Muddy Waters, Buddy Guy, or his lesser known brother Phil Guy.

Later on in the album, Rory takes a bow to the folk music of America and the Blue Ridge Highway of Doc Watson on 'Out of My Mind'. He shows his astonishing grasp of acoustic finger picking, which he was keen to say in interviews down through the decades he was constantly working on throughout his career.

'Crest of A Wave', in effect, describes where he saw his role as a musician and artist. Constantly developing, no matter what the disciplines or energies, he was always on the crest of that wave. His slide playing on this track in particular is sublime and effortless but also has that troubled sound that only a fine player can achieve.

Rory spoke to Pat Egan about the making of the album. 'I was looking for a raw earthy sound on *Deuce* and I was fairly pleased with it. *Deuce* made the top twenty for one week, I guess I was a little disappointed but not depressed, after all 17,000 albums is not bad. If I can find a suitable venue we will definitely do a live recording soon, though it may not be the next release.' Rory was wrong, and his next release would be the remarkable *Live in Europe*. In the meantime, however, there came the chance to play with a musical legend.

APPRECIATION SOCIETY

DEUCE

INTRO. ISSUE

This is the cover of the introductory edition of the Rory Gallagher Appreciation Society fanzine Deuce, which was edited by Julie Gordon (courtesy Gordon Morris).

Starlight magazine, the successor to *Spotlight*, in 1978 with Rory proclaiming that glam rock was not for him.

Moving On – a strange yet unique album sleeve from Polydor Germany, repackaging a Taste album.

T'S A RARE THING to meet your heroes in life, rarer still to sit down and play guitar with them. But that is exactly what happened to Rory Gallagher, in December 1971, when he got a call from Esmond Edwards of Chess Records to join the session band for *Muddy Waters – The London Sessions*.

In his foreword to Sandra B. Tooze's *Muddy Waters: The Mojo Man*, Eric Clapton described how 'The blues is not about self-pity or self-indulgence, it's about courage in the face of adversity, the truth of the soul, and the nobility of the spirit in its infinite capacity to suffer and rejoice at exactly the same time. How, you may ask, do I know all this? Because I have listened to Muddy Waters all of my life, and this is what his music taught me.'

Clapton continued in a reverential tone: 'I eventually got to meet Muddy and got to know him pretty well, and to me he was like a tribal chief, a Buddha, and a naughty boy all rolled into one, but what I remember most about him was his dignity. In response to his own personal vision, Muddy took the music of the Delta plantation, transplanted it into a Chicago night club, surrounded it with an electric band and proceeded to change the course of popular music forever. In doing so, I believe Muddy became one of the most significant links between early African-American culture and the global electronics of modern rock and roll as we know it today. For myself, nothing can compare with the eerie combination of his slide and voice on songs like "Walkin' Blues" or "I Feel Like Going Home". His music changed my life, and whether you know it or not, and like it or not, it probably changed yours too.'

Muddy Waters, from his discovery on Stovall's Plantation by Alan Lomax, as part of the Library of Congress Archive of Folk Song Project in 1941, through to his first visit to Chicago and the remarkable legacy of recordings he made for Chess Records, was a colossus of American blues. By the early 1970s, however, young players like Buddy Guy, Johnny Winter, and Jimi Hendrix were overtaking his place in the blues pantheon. He was also suffering from serious injuries picked up in a car crash in October 1969, when the car he was travelling in – a new Chevy station wagon – collided with an oncoming Pontiac, driven by a young couple on Highway 45 near Urbana, Illinois. Four people died – the young couple and two members of the band. Muddy's friend, Andrew 'Bo' Bolton, travelling behind, came to the rescue of the injured. James 'Pee Wee' Madison, the guitarist, was 'smashed up against the windscreen'. Bolton and another musician, Sammy Lawhorn, then pulled Willie 'Pinetop' Perkins and Muddy out of the back of the car and laid them on the grass. They were both conscious but badly injured. Muddy's injuries included three broken ribs, a fractured pelvis, a shattered hip and back sprain. He was hospitalised for three months.

Muddy Waters – The London Sessions was a response by the legendary Chess Records to a huge wave of interest in the blues from artists on this side of the Atlantic, including Eric Clapton, the Rolling Stones, John Mayall's Bluesbreakers, Fleetwood Mac, and our very own Rory Gallagher, who first heard Muddy Waters on the American Forces Network, broadcasting from Germany. The session band was a mix of the finest blues players from this side of the pond – Rory on guitar, Rick Grech on bass, Steve Winwood on piano/organ, Georgie Fame on piano/organ, and Mitch Mitchell on drums – together with a coterie of Chicago blues veterans – Sam Lawhorn on guitar, Carey Bell Harrington on harmonica (or 'Mississippi saxophone'), Herbie Lovelle on drums, Rosetta Hightower on vocals, Ernie Royal and Joe Newman on trumpets, Garnett Brown on trombone, and Seldon Powell on tenor saxophone. The 58-year-old Muddy Waters was on vocals and slide guitar. The album was recorded over a short space of time, from Saturday 4 to Wednesday 8 December, and released in April 1972.

It was an easy atmosphere as a lot of the musicians knew each other well and were familiar with one another's styles. Grech and Winwood had both played with Blind Faith, the supergroup Taste had supported on tour in America. Mitch Mitchell and Georgie Fame, meanwhile, had served together in Georgie Fame and the Blue Flames, before Mitch joined the remarkable Jimi Hendrix Experience behind the kit. For Rory, it was one of the most remarkable periods of his life. 'The whole thing stuck in my memory like a video. I can plug it in at any time and replay it in my head. I only wish that I could do it again with my experience now because Muddy taught me an awful lot during those recording sessions and I came out a much better player than I went in.

'I used to have to play gigs in different parts of the country in the evenings and then, afterwards, we'd drive up to the IBC Studios in London for the recordings and they would hold up the sessions until

I arrived. So I'd finish in, say, Birmingham or Bristol at 10.30 pm and then I'd jump in the car and drive like the devil to get there as soon as I could. Muddy would be sitting there with his glass and a cigar. He'd give me a glass of red wine when I arrived and we would start playing at midnight or 1.00 am, which is my time of day. That was more than polite, I just seemed to get on well with him and we laid down quite a few tracks.

'I learned a lot watching him tune his guitar, and watching the way he sang and performed. I mean, just to be working in close quarters with him, even if it was only three nights, was quite an experience. What made it somewhat easier than I had imagined was that many of the songs that we did were songs he had recorded before, like "I'm Ready". There was also "I'm Gonna Move to the Outskirts of Town", which he hadn't recorded before, and "Who's Gonna Be Your Sweet Man When I'm Gone" and "Young Fashioned Ways". The hardest thing was to get the drums and bass guitar in sync with Muddy's type of rhythm guitar. We had Sammy Lawhorn there on guitar, along with me, so it would be in a fairly confined fashion; it wasn't lead guitar all over the place. Muddy played slide on two of the tracks and he would play on some tracks with the guitar strapped on him and plant a little riff someplace. The production was fairly loose and there were ideas coming from a fellah called Esmond Edwards from Chess Records.'

Esmond Edwards was an interesting character in his own right. Although born in Kingston, Jamaica, he grew up in Harlem, New York City, developing an interest in photography and taking shots of local musicians and dancers that were published in *The New York Times*. Initially hired as a clerk at Prestige Records, Edwards worked his way up the ladder to become head of the jazz label Verve in 1967. Edwards was one of the first African-Americans to hold such a high-ranking position within the recording industry. In 1970, Edwards moved to Chicago to take on the position of vice president of Artist & Repertoire (A&R) for Chess Records, collaborating with blues legends such as Muddy Waters, Chuck Berry, and B. B. King. Edwards' photographs grace the sleeves of countless classic jazz albums and he left a legacy of remarkable images of African-American musicians and composers.

'We did another new song, "Blind Man Blues",' Rory continued, 'and I can remember a couple of times Muddy would stop the song if he didn't like the way it was going. But a few suggestions were made by Steve Winwood on organ or Georgie Fame on piano. As

Rory on the docks in Cork in the 1980s,
sitting astride the Ford (© Colm Henry).

with a lot of these kinds of sessions there's not all that much verbal communication, you know, a lot of it's just stop and start again, can you pick that up or can you start in a different key.

'Just watching him tuning his guitar or doing something like "Walkin' Blues" was wonderful for me, and the great thing about the *London Sessions* was that it wasn't just a 'token' blues legend with a load of Europeans. Muddy had his own musicians as well, with Carey Bell on harp [harmonica], Sam Lawhorn on guitar. They were magical nights.

'Muddy had great strength of character. He was always very polite and he could also be very powerful if he did not like something. He could do it with the click of his fingers, without causing an argument or ruining the atmosphere. He would just quietly say to the drummer – either Mitch Mitchell or Herbie Lovelle – "pick it up a wee bit there" and it happened.

'He had a lovely Buddha-like countenance, great authority. You knew he was in charge of things but you could also make suggestions to him. Georgie Fame suggested a few things and so did I and he always listened. This was the early 1970s and he still had a few years to live. It was a few years after the car crash and his back was bad. He was often in great pain but never got nasty, that wasn't his nature at all.

'After the recordings we drove him back to his hotel a couple of times. I've kept that car ever since, as a sort of shrine, because Muddy sat in it. It's an old Ford Executive, a real *Hawaii Five-O* car, with tail fins and stars and stripes down the side. It's sitting at home in front of our house in Cork. The car is falling apart at the seams but I refuse to scrap it or anything. I can still see Muddy in the front seat, smoking those cigars with a big plastic tip on them. I only wish I'd had a Super 8 camera to capture all that stuff. I know one of the guys from Chicago took some shots and I'd love to get them for my grandchildren, if I ever have grandchildren. It's a beautiful memory for me.'

Sadly, the Ford Executive is no more. It languished outside the family home in Douglas for many years, and although several plans were mooted to attempt its restoration they came to nought. Muddy Waters, the great Buddha of the blues, died in April 1983 at the Good Samaritan Hospital in Downers Grove, Illinois. The Father of Chicago blues was no more.

Live In Europe

Rory revisits the Shandon Boat Club, Cork (© Colm Henry).

ORY GREW UP during the British 'blues boom' of the 1960s and his preoccupation with the blues and African-American bluesmen was nothing short of remarkable. He did not like some sides to the blues boom. 'If there was one fault with the boom in the 1960s, it was that it was very straight-faced and very pontificatory, or whatever the word is. It used to annoy me that there was an attitude of "Thou shalt not play the blues unless you know who played second acoustic guitar behind Sonny Boy Williamson the first on the B-side of whatever." That kind of thing gets music nowhere, it's like collecting stamps. I mean, I buy books on the blues and I check out the B-sides and I know who plays on what records and that's fine. But then you've got to open that up to the rest of the people. Because that kind of snobbery defeats the purpose; it kills the music.'

Live in Europe, released in 1972, showcased Rory's great knowledge of the blues. It opens with Mel London's 'Messin' With The Kid', recorded by Junior Wells in Chicago. This would become one of Rory's signature tunes. Junior Wells was born Amos Blackwell in Memphis, Tennessee, on 9 December 1934, in John Gaston Hospital. He was a self-taught harmonica player who was sitting in with Tampa Red before he turned twenty. He formed a trio with Dave and Louis Myers called the Three Deuces and later guested with Muddy Waters in the Ebony Lounge in Chicago. Just a few years later, he was to replace Little Walter in Muddy's band, working local club dates around Chicago in the early 1950s.

Junior joined the US Army and served between 1953 and 1955. On his return to Chicago after military service, he recorded with Muddy for Chess Records. Junior was a 'harp for hire' and, by 1958, he had become a regular sideman in Buddy Guy's band, working Peppers Lounge, Theresa's Lounge, and the Blue Flame Club at a time when the blues was around every corner on the southside of Chicago. Junior Wells recorded 'Messin' With The Kid' on 17 October 1960 with Earl Hooker, another hero of Rory's, on lead guitar, Lacey Gibson on rhythm guitar, Johnny Walker on piano, the remarkable Fred Below on drums, Jack Myers on bass, Jarrett Gibson on tenor saxophone, Donald Hankins on baritone saxophone, and Wells on vocals and harmonica, with Mel London producing.

Mel London, born in Mississippi in 1932, was the owner of Chicago label Chief Records, which issued the original version of his composition 'Messin' with the Kid' in 1960. The song became a staple of blues combos and was covered by Luther Allison, John Mayall and his Bluesbreakers, Johnny Winter, Buddy Guy, Detroit Junior, Freddie King, The Blues Brothers, and Eddie C. Campbell. The most unlikely cover was by the band from Warwickshire in England, the Edgar Broughton Blues Band, who later morphed into the psychedelic rock band The Edgar Broughton Band. It was included on their album *Wasa Wasa*. The Edgar Broughton Band was a great puzzle for the creatives in EMI Records so they established a psychedelic label, Harvest, which became home to Deep Purple with the release of their second album *The Book of Taliesyn*, Shirley and Dolly Collins, Tea and Symphony, The Third Ear Band, Pete Brown and his Battered Ornaments, and later Piblokto, Michael Chapman, Roy Harper, Syd Barrett, and Barclay James Harvest. The jewel in the crown was Pink Floyd, who had taken their name from two obscure bluesmen Pink Anderson and Floyd Jones.

Rory had, by now, established himself as a major force throughout Europe. His favourite venue on tour was the Olympia in Paris. *Live in Europe* was recorded on the road during February and March of 1972, playing venues in Germany, Holland and Belgium. The album captures the essence of Gallagher's live performance, which he himself would readily admit was rarely captured in the recording studio, with the possible exceptions of *Against the Grain* and *Tattoo* and, most certainly, his final studio album released in 1990 *Fresh Evidence*.

The second track on the album is an extrapolated version of 'Laundromat' from his first solo album, which had become a firm stage favourite. It's followed by 'I Could've Had Religion', Rory's salute to the 'redemption style blues', as he termed it, of Reverend Robert Wilkins and Reverend Gary Davis, with a soft opening on guitar and harmonica building to a slow twelve bar blues, with Gerry McAvoy and Wilgar Campbell providing the solid rhythm section. Many years later, Bob Dylan expressed interest in the track, suspecting it was an obscure traditional blues and not realising it was in fact penned by Rory although credited by him to the blues sources that drove his writing.

The Reverend Robert Wilkins was born in Hernando, Mississippi, on 16 January 1896. After serving in the US army in the First World War, he moved to Memphis, Tennessee. A self-taught guitarist, Reverend Wilkins is described by Francis Davis in *The History of the Blues: The*

Roots, The Music, The People as a musician 'who fit the popular image of a Delta bluesman as a performer between conjure and the cross, though in truth he was different from most of his contemporaries in every way. Wilkins was ordained as a minister in the late 1940s in the Church of God in Christ and became a practitioner in herbal medicine. He was a lifelong teetotaller, scornful of much of the loose behaviour he witnessed in the juke joints and was shaken by the frequent outbursts of violence that occurred in them ... Before Wilkins abandoned secular music his songs were those of a man wondering if he was on the right path. They were such polished little gems that it's surprising so few of them have been reinterpreted by other performers – especially in light of the fact that The Rolling Stones covered his "That's No Way To Get Along" as "Prodigal Son" on the album *Beggar's Banquet*. (Wilkins recorded a two-part blues in 1928 called "Rollin' Stone".) Wilkins was one of the many elderly performers unearthed by revivalists in the 1960s, but when persuaded to record again, he insisted on making an album of gospel songs – no blues.' Wilkins died on 26 May 1987 in Memphis.

'Pistol Slapper Blues', the next track, was written by Fulton Allen – or Blind Boy Fuller as he is better known. It was originally recorded on 5 April 1938 in New York City with Blind Boy Fuller on vocals and guitar and Sonny Terry on harmonica. One of Rory's great sources for his blues were the Carolinas. Blind Boy Fuller was born in 1907 near the state line between North and South Carolina in Wadesboro, Anson County. Unlike many of his later contemporaries, he didn't come from a musical family. While his sister, Ethel, played guitar, the young Fulton Allen had only a passing interest in music in his teenage years. In the mid-1920s his mother died and his father Calvin moved the family east to Rockingham. Fuller met Cora Mae Martin here. They married when he was just nineteen years old and she a mere fourteen. Fuller developed an eye problem in Rockingham, but when he consulted a doctor in Charlotte he was of little help. As many at this time were migrant workers, Fuller and his new bride, Cora Mae, moved north to Winston-Salem. Fuller found work in a local coal yard for a time. Soon, though, his eyesight gave him so much irritation and trouble that he could not function at work and became dependent on Cora Mae who had just turned sixteen. They moved east to Durham next to avail of whatever form of limited social services were available to someone who was visually impaired.

Although Fuller was not completely blind until 1928, he really applied himself to what Cora Mae referred to as 'the box', which he'd practice all day long. Living in Durham, he also came under the spell of the Reverend Gary Davis (Blind Gary Davis). In 1933, like so many others in his predicament, Fuller was given a permit to busk on the streets of Durham. It's rumoured he made a decent living from this life as a vaudevillian and before long came to the notice of a local store owner J. B. Long. Long had, for some time, been a talent scout for the American Record Company and he felt that they should record Fuller. So began the career of Blind Boy Fuller. In July 1935, the white store owner Long drove Fuller and local washboard player Bull City Red to New York to record. They were joined there by Gary Davis. The recording supervisor, according to Bruce Bastin in *Red River Blues*, his guide to the blues of the Carolinas, was Arthur Edward Satherley, known as Art Satherley. Working at Paramount Records from 1918 to 1929, Art had gained a wide range of knowledge and experience, much of this with rural and African-American performers, marketing what were termed 'race records' at that time. Art then joined Plaza Music, which was taken over by the American Record Corporation. Blind Boy Fuller and Gary Davis were extremely fortunate that they were in a recording studio for their first session with one of the most experienced A&R men of the time, and one with a breadth of experience and understanding of the blues idiom.

Gary Davis was born on 30 April 1896 in Laurens, South Carolina, the son of a farmhand. Although almost blind from infancy, he taught himself the harmonica by the age of five, banjo by the time he was six, and guitar at seven. He attended the Cedar Springs School for Blind People in Spartanburg, South Carolina, and by 1926, he had lost his sight entirely. The following year he headed north to North Carolina and the more prosperous cities of Durham and Asheville, settling, after a number of years, in Durham where he encountered Blind Boy Fuller. Performing as musicians was one of the few occupations open to visually impaired bluesmen. Many of them started playing during the tobacco harvesting season and this would have been the reason behind Davis travelling north to Durham, Raleigh, Asheville, and Winston-Salem. With the workers being paid at the end of the harvest, players like Blind Boy Fuller and Davis made the most of the opportunity.

In 1940, Gary Davis was ordained a minister in the Missionary Baptist Connection Church and made the move to New York City, working on street corners as a singing preacher and performing at folk concerts and on local radio. Around 1945 he recorded for Moses Asch and secured a job teaching at Brownie McGhee's Home of the Blues Music School. He performed at the Leadbelly Memorial Concert in New York's Town Hall in 1950 and in 1954 recorded for the Stinson label – a label that recorded the late Patrick Galvin, the distinguished Cork writer and poet, in an album of folk songs. Davis made many visits to Europe in the 1960s with the Blues Caravan and played all the major festivals, recording for a range of labels. Reverend Gary Davis is a towering figure in the blues pantheon through his playing and writing of such classics as 'Cocaine Blues', 'You've Got to Move', and 'Candyman'. He was a major influence on Ry Cooder, Donovan Leitch, Bob Dylan, Stefan Grossman, Larry Johnson, Brownie McGhee, Ralph McTell, Taj Mahal, Dave van Ronk, and Eric Clapton. Davis died, following a heart attack, en route to a concert date in New Jersey in May 1972.

The standout track on the *Live in Europe* album for any Gallagher fan has to be 'Going to My Hometown', where he name checks Ford's famous car factory and Dunlop Tyres, both huge employers in Cork at the time. The call and response especially on the swaying floor timbers of Cork City Hall on his Irish tours are never to be forgotten.

When the CD version of this album was issued in 1999, two bonus tracks were added, 'What in the World' and 'Hoodoo Man'. The album closes with 'Bullfrog Blues', written by William Harris and a staple of Gallagher's live set for the next three decades. Rory may well have discovered the original recording on the album *Delta Blues Heavy Hitters, 1927–1931*, featuring Skip James, Blind Joe Reynolds, and Harris. Paul Oliver describes this album as a 'must have' in the *Blackwell Guide to Essential Blues Recordings*. Harris, he writes, was 'one of the most rhythmically powerful folk blues artists ever recorded and sings with a beautiful, rich voice'.

Live in Europe was a major commercial success for Rory, his first solo top ten album chart entry. It eventually secured him his first Gold Disc, of which many more were to come. That same year – 1972 – also saw *Melody Maker* honour him as Guitarist/Musician of the Year.

DOMINION THEATRE, Tottenham Court Rd.

Asgard presents—

Guitarists Night

SATURDAY **24** Evening 8.00
MARCH Doors open 7.30

STALLS
£6.00

D 30

B. Cooper (Printers) Ltd., Chorlton Manchester

Nº 8024

STRANGE MUSIC
presents

RORY GALLAGHER
& HIS BAND
+ Guests

A Sense
of Ireland

Lyceum, Strand, London, WC2
MONDAY 17th MARCH at 7.30 p.m.
£4.00 (including V.A.T.)

THE DOME, BRIGHTON

FRIDAY
19th SEPTEMBER, 1980
at 7.30 p.m.

Rory Gallagher
ROW

E 28

STALLS

including VAT £3.50

Tickets cannot be accepted for exchange
or refund. Latecomers will not have access
to their seats until a suitable interval.
TO BE RETAINED

FREE TRADE HALL Peter St., Manchester

Derek Block presents—

Rory Gallagher
IN CONCERT

Tuesday, 16th December, 1975 at 7.30 p.m.

*No money refunds or ticket exchanges. Official Brochures
sold ONLY in the Theatre.*

CENTRE CIRCLE £2.20 inc. VAT

F 15

ABC Printers, Manchester

RETAIN THIS PORTION

VICTORIA HALL, HANLEY

TUESDAY, 7th OCTOBER, 1980
at 7.30 p.m.

Strange Music presents

RORY
GALLAGHER
AND HIS BAND
PLUS GUESTS

THIS PORTION TO BE RETAINED
BY THE PURCHASER
NO TICKET CAN BE EXCHANGED
OR MONEY REFUNDED

Ticket Unreserved
£3.50
(including V.A.T.)

Nº 78

Official Merchandise is
only on sale inside the
Hall.
Cameras, Tape Recorders
and Alcohol of any sort
will not be allowed into
the venue.
The Management reserve the right to
refuse admission.
NO PASSOUTS

MIKE LLOYD (MUSIC) LTD.
15, Percy Street, Hanley 24641
23, High Street, Newcastle 610940
109, High Street, Tunstall 84660

QUARRY PROMOTIONS
PRESENT

RORY GALLAGHER
AND HIS BAND
at the
NATIONAL EXHIBITION CENTRE, BIRMINGHAM
PLUS GUEST SUPPORT

SATURDAY, 9th DECEMBER, 1978
Doors open 6.30 p.m.

£3·50 HALL 6
including VAT 2587

CONDITIONS OF SALE: Advertised programmes are
subject to alteration. Tickets cannot be exchanged nor
money refunded. The management reserve the right to
refuse admission.
For train service details see over.

RORY GALLAGHER'S NEXT ALBUM, *Blueprint*, was released in early 1973. The recording took place in the recently re-vamped Marquee Studios and in Polydor's in-house studio complex. Rory produced the album himself and the engineers were Phil Dunn and Andy Stephens. The original album cover featured the circuit board drawings for a Stramp 'Power Baby' Amplifier, which was a standard piece of Rory's stage equipment. This particular drawing was of a custom built model designed for Rory in Hamburg. 'It was compact enough to fit into the small luggage compartment of a Volkswagen Beetle,' remembered Donal Gallagher.

The tracks on the album included 'Bankers Blues', composed by Big Bill Broonzy, and 'Daughter of the Everglades', a salute to the swamp and zydeco music of Louisiana that Rory would revisit in 1990 on *Fresh Evidence*, with his tribute to Clifton Chenier – the King of Zydeco.

The revised line-up for *Blueprint* saw two former members of the blues band Killing Floor joining Rory, with Rod De'Ath replacing Wilgar Campbell on drums and Lou Martin from Belfast joining on keyboards.

I interviewed Lou at the Burnley Blues Festival in 1999, where he was playing keyboards with long-time accomplice Mick Clarke. They played straight ahead Chicago blues in the style of Muddy Waters and Jimmy Rogers. Lou, when he joined the ranks of Rory's band, took on the role held by Muddy's piano man, Otis Spann.

'I grew up in Belfast and when I was ten the family moved to England. My early music interests were in classical piano, attending music school, and when I came to London I went to Trinity College studying piano with the intention of teaching. By the time I was fourteen that all went out the window because I started seeing rhythm and blues bands – Spencer Davis and John Mayall played around the place, and I thought nah … I don't want to teach, I want to play this. I tracked down the records, which were not that easy to find. I found out about B. B. King and Muddy by going to hear the Bluesbreakers and hearing Eric Clapton talking about them and wondering where's that guitar sound coming from … who's Freddie King? … who's Otis Rush? … Jesse Fuller? So when I got hold of these records, it was a case of just sticking them on the turntable with the piano in the front room and I just sort of played along with them.

'My greatest pleasure in those years was tracking down Jimmy

Reed records and obscure Muddy Waters and just sitting at home and listening for hours on end. In my first band with Mick Clarke, Killing Floor, we used to play the Marquee about once every six weeks on Tuesday blues night or whatever ... Around the time Taste broke up, I was living with Rod De'Ath, the drummer with Killing Floor. We were sort of living in a commune in a house in Streatham ... This was real "hippy" days, but Rod decided that he might let the top room of the house out, so he put an ad in the *London Evening Standard* and who turned up on the doorstep on the Saturday night but this guy in a suit and tie and everything like that.

'He turned around to me and started talking with a broad Belfast accent. It happened to be Gerry McAvoy, you know? And we sort of brought him in and he saw all the band gear in the hall. "Oh, band is it?" he says. "Oh aye," I said. "Well what kind of band?" "Oh, we're a blues band ... you don't play in a band?" (He was, after all, all dressed up). Says Gerry "No, I just put the suit on for the ... I thought I was going to have a landlord, you know."

'We explained the room upstairs, twenty-five bob a week, and he said "I play with Rory Gallagher" and I nearly freaked, looked at him and said, "Christ, you don't." "Oh, it's true, it's true ... I've come over here from Belfast to do an album and do some gigs."

'So as time went on Gerry eventually sort of said, "Well, maybe you'd like to come along to a gig," and so I said "Yeah, I'd love it," 'cause we were doing Fairfield Hall in Croydon when he was doing the Festival Hall, Killing Floor went along to it. I went backstage and met himself and Rory, this was 1971 and a few weeks went by and we were doing a gig at the Marquee and Gerry had a night off so he brought the whole entourage down ... Donal, Rory, they all came down. Rory really liked what we were doing at the time ... so the connection was being made ... like hanging around the bar at the Marquee and nattering to him and so I found out "Christ! This guy is into Jimmy Rogers and Chicago stuff." Then Wilgar Campbell suddenly became ill and the band needed a drummer at short notice. The only other drummer that Rory knew was suitable was Rod De'Ath, so Rod joined the band ... after a while Rory mentioned to Rod while they were out on the road that he "wouldn't mind experimenting with a keyboard player, you might bring your mate that played the Marquee down for a jam" ... A few days later he rang. "I'd like you to come along and play my numbers", which I kind of knew anyway, and then he said,

"I'd like you to come to Italy" and then "Come to the States with us and maybe it could be an ongoing situation" … I mean I didn't even have a passport at the time, it was just sort of "Yes, ok you're on", and that basically was it, it was all done over mutual chats over pints of Guinness, the business was completely a side issue … Rory was a year older than me, but when we talked we compared record collections like "Well, I've got this Jimmy Rogers's album *Chicago Bound*" or "Would you like 'Sloppy Drunk' or stuff like that or do you like 'I'm Going to Main Street' and 'That's Alright'.

'Albums were always done in a rush because we were on the road so much, and then we'd come back to London and it could be two weeks – like *Blueprint* was done in two weeks – and that is ridiculous, I mean so we'd like put it together quickly. We didn't get down to recording some decent stuff until the latter days of *Tattoo*, but *Irish Tour* was an absolute highlight, the version of "I Wonder Who", I rate that version so much, the band came to fruition in the *Calling Card* days, by that time we were well seasoned … everybody knew everybody else's style of playing. I wanted him to play more blues, he wanted me to play more blues, like you know Leroy Carr/Francis "Scrapper" Blackwell thing. Actually "Bankers Blues" stands out as a very early example, that's one of the best tracks on *Blueprint*.'

The studio was not the best environment for recording. 'He wasn't at his most comfortable or happiest, I mean a lot of people really adapted to it really well like The Allman Brothers or Little Feat. With Rory, if he didn't have somebody to look at then he couldn't feed off the energy. That's why *Irish Tour* is such a good bloody album because it was recorded live, he got the crowd there with him singing along and sort of like urging him along … without the presence of an audience the recording process for Rory was a bit of a strain, particularly after two hours or more in studio.'

13
Canada

Theo Reijnder's painting of Rory.

THE BEGINNING OF 1973 found Rory touring Germany again before returning to London to record an 'In Concert' special for the BBC. Rory had a very strong and trusting relationship with BBC Radio, whether with Mike Raven in the Taste days or the remarkable John Peel whose radio show played Taste's very first single. In February 1973, Rory recorded 'Hands Off' and 'Race the Breeze' for John Peel mid-week and they were mixed down and broadcast a few days later. You can hear examples of the quality of the playing and the care taken by the BBC sound engineers and producers on the double CD *Rory Gallagher – BBC Sessions*, which was issued by the BBC and Donal Gallagher in 1999, with twenty-two tracks ranging from 'Calling Card' to 'Hoodoo Man'.

Rory, who had just turned twenty-five, and the re-jigged band then played some Canadian dates in March 1973. It was the guitarist's first time returning to Toronto since Taste had supported Blind Faith in 1969. The shows in Toronto were reported in the British music press. Jim Smith of the *New Musical Express*, which was overtaking its main rival *Melody Maker* in importance, filed this review from the city for the magazine's 7 April issue:

'One week ago I barely knew the name Rory Gallagher. In my defence, it should be pointed out that he's not yet the star in North America that he is in Britain. His *Live in Europe* album has sold some eighty thousand copies in America – a respectable sale, but not enough to put him on the front pages. Still I heard good reports of him from Lori Burner, the local Polydor promotion rep (and one of the best on this continent), and decided to pass up Duke Ellington and Fats Domino (both playing in town) to see this wonder kid.

'And the verdict? Gallagher really is exceptionally talented.

'Fortunately for Gallagher, not everyone in Toronto was as uninformed as me. For the full week Rory spent at the Colonial Tavern (Toronto's leading Jazz and Blues club), there wasn't an empty seat.

'Monday night is traditionally a throwaway night, when the waiters outnumber the patrons. But Rory had standing-room only, and let it also be noted that the Colonial is not small. By the weekend, even the other record companies were talking about Gallagher. There was a queue on Saturday evening a full hour before his first set.

'Yeah, Rory did all right for himself.

'The audience didn't do too badly for itself either. Gallagher played like there would be no tomorrow. Seventy-five-minute sets at a minimum (twice a night) and encores as well. Rory loved it; his musicians were exhausted. Later he told me that wasn't a lot of work: "When we played Hamburg in the 1960s, my fingers were bleeding at the end of the night."

'Apart from his hard work, the other half of his greatness is his ability. For the past year, I've been spending a lot of time around B. B. King; that kind of association really spoils a person when it comes to listening to other guitarists. Except for T-Bone Walker, there aren't many who can really turn me on. Gallagher got to me.

'For his age, he's a superb guitarist. There are only a few flaws in his stage presence, but that all takes care of itself with time. His voice isn't exceptional. But he throws himself into his music with such abandon that he should lose control; he never does though. He chords and picks equally well.

'Most guitarists of any repute carry a second guitarist to handle the chording, leaving them to pick the lead notes (and pick up the glamour). Gallagher does everything himself, filling in where there should, by rights, be gaps (after all, he is only one man).

'I also found his diversified styles intriguing, he picks rather like B. B. at times, chords like nobody I've heard, and throws in touches of bottle-neck guitar. By rights, Gallagher's group should not be interesting; after all, there are only the four of them – Rory; drummer – Rod De'Ath; pianist – Lou Martin; and bassist Gerry McAvoy – and they haven't been together all that long. However, they are interesting and not solely because of Gallagher. Gallagher is a high energy guitarist, of course, but he is always in control. His sidemen share the same characteristics. The result is loud but graceful instead of the primitive rush of noise I've heard from too many other high-energy bands (including, incidentally, Deep Purple, a band Rory will be travelling with for part of his current tour).

'The most fascinating aspect of Gallagher, to me anyway, is his potential. He says he intends keeping up the pace for another twenty years. If he can, the possibilities are staggering; after all B. B. King and T-Bone Walker were in their late thirties before they came into their own.'

Smith went on to write about the act sharing the bill with Rory.

'The Gallagher show was interesting in another respect. Sharing the bill was King Biscuit Boy – Richard Newell himself. Newell is loaded with talent. Unfortunately, he's rather short on drive, because since Christmas ('72) he's been in virtual retirement. The Gallagher date was in fact his first job since then. With that kind of lay-off, King Biscuit Boy should have been rusty. But I've never heard him in better form. Part of the reason was undoubtedly Mainline, the back-up band, who pushed him to better performances time and again. He may be going back on the road soon. I hope so. He is a born performer and a genuine talent.'

As a result of reading this review I went out and got my hands on a copy of King Biscuit Boy's album and *Stink* by McKenna Mendelson Mainline, or Mainline as they were called on those dates in the Colonial Tavern in Toronto when Rory certainly left his mark on music critic Jim Smith. Rory would return to Canada regularly throughout the 1970s, one of his favourite venues being the legendary El Mocambo in Toronto.

THROUGHOUT THE 1970s, Rory was much called upon as a high-premium session musician, playing, for example, on the Mike Vernon album *Bring it Back Home*, which was recorded and released in 1971. Vernon, doyenne of the late 1960s British blues boom, had already produced seminal recordings by Fleetwood Mac, Savoy Brown, Duster Bennett, John Mayall and the Bluesbreakers, Chicken Shack, and Ten Years After for his own label Blue Horizon. The rest of the line-up for this album were Rory Gallagher and Paul Kossoff of Free on lead guitars, Rick Hayward on guitar, Dick Parry on sax, and Pete Wingfield on piano. Rory also cropped up on an early concept album by Mike Batt called *Tarot Suite*. Rory worked with yet another of his boyhood heroes, Lonnie Donegan, one of the founding fathers of skiffle, on the album *Puttin' on the Style*.

In 1973, Rory was called up by producer Steve Rowland to work on another *London Sessions* outing, this time with the dangerous man of rock 'n' roll – Jerry Lee Lewis. The rest of the stellar line-up included Tony Ashton of Deep Purple, Delaney Bramlett, pedal steel guitarist B. J. Cole, Tony Colton, Pete Gavin, Chas Hodges, ace guitarist Albert Lee of Heads, Hands and Feet, Alvin Lee of Ten Years After, Kenny Jones, and Mickey Jones. The album also featured Drew Croon and Matthew Fisher, John Gustafson, Klaus Voorman, Gary Wright, Gary Taylor, and backing vocalists Thunderthighs – Karen Friedman, Dari Lallou, and Casey Synge.

The album, released on the Mercury label, opened with a number Jerry Lee had played at his first public performance with a country

This publicity still for Mercury Records shows Rory and Jerry Lee Lewis 'The Killer' in studio for a London Sessions.

Jerry Lee Lewis reclines at the piano as (l–r) guitarists Albert Lee, Peter Frampton and Rory Gallagher lay down the track with Kenny Jones on drums.

and western band on the lot of a Ford dealership, an R&B classic from 1949 called 'Drinking Wine Spo-Dee O Dee', which was composed by Sticks McGhee. Lewis, who was born in Ferriday, Louisiana, on 29 September 1935, picked up the nickname of 'The Killer' in the schoolyard. A wild child, he married first at sixteen and epitomises, along with Elvis Presley, the essence of rock and roll. He recorded first for Sam Philips' Sun Record label in Memphis with Cowboy Jack Clement. His first single was a cover version of a Ray Price country hit 'Crazy Arms'. He toured with Johnny Cash and Carl Perkins and they felt he was too reserved so the following night on the tour he stood at the piano, kicked the stool away, and used his foot on the keys ... 'The Killer' had arrived. At his next studio recording, he made 'Whole Lotta Shakin' Goin On'. This was followed by 'Great Balls of Fire', 'Breathless', and 'High School Confidential' in the late 1950s. His only hit, however, through the 1960s was a cover version of Ray Charles' 'What'd I Say'.

The *London Sessions* was a double album in an ornate gate-fold sleeve. Other tracks included Creedence Clearwater Revival's 'Bad Moon Rising', written by John Fogerty, leading country singer and composer Charlie Rich's 'No Headstone On My Grave', two tracks written by Jimmy Reed, 'Baby What You Want Me To Do' and 'Big Boss Man', and Chuck Berry's classics 'Memphis' and 'Johnny Be Goode'. Guest musician Tony Colton contributed 'Music to the Man'; he also co-wrote 'Jukebox' alongside Ray Smith, Albert Lee, and Chas Hodges. Lewis also covered Little Richard's 'Jenny, Jenny', 'Long Tall Sally', and 'Tutti Frutti'.

Rory recalled for Liam Fay of *Hot Press* how Jerry Lee behaved: 'There was a strange sense of violence and madness around whenever Jerry Lee Lewis was in the room. Whenever anyone annoyed him, he'd immediately pull up his left trouser leg and go for his sock as if he had a gun in it. I never actually saw him with a gun in the studio but I'm sure if he'd had one, he'd have shot somebody. There was always a borderline of danger about him which I think is necessary for real rock and roll.'

A year after the release of the *Jerry Lee Lewis – London Sessions*, Rory's words proved to be somewhat prophetic. Rory and a few friends were invited to a special Jerry Lee Lewis showcase gig in the Roxy in Los Angeles in 1974. Also at the concert on the night was John Lennon (a declared Taste fan in the 1960s). Rory recalled the night:

'Lennon was going through his LA phase at the time, his hair was really short but everyone still recognised him and they all turned around to look at him as he took his seat on the balcony of the Roxy. Needless to say, the fact that he was being "upstaged" drove Jerry Lee wild. He started to do the "Jerry Lee Rag" but everybody was still looking up at Lennon and whispering about him. All of a sudden, Jerry Lee stopped and started on about how The Beatles were "shit" and the Stones were "shit" and there ain't nobody could play real rock n' roll the way Jerry Lee could. Lennon loved this, he had his boot up on the balcony and he started egging Jerry Lee on, shouting "yeah, you're right there, man, The Beatles are shit". People started laughing but Jerry Lee thought that Lennon was shouting abuse at him, so he freaked out altogether. He just pushed the piano across the stage and stormed off.

'The atmosphere in the Roxy was tense, most people left the venue, fearing that Jerry Lee might go on the rampage with one of the firearms that everyone knew he always carried with him, others stuck around to see what might happen.'

Rory had a backstage pass and wanted to go into Jerry Lee's dressing room to try to cheer him up and attempt to calm him down. Rory's brother and manager, Donal, warned against this course of action and cautioned that Rory would be risking his life to enter such a fearsome lion's den at a time like this. Enter at this delicate juncture Tom O'Driscoll, the gentle giant from Schull in west Cork. A former fisherman by trade, Tom was ever present in the Gallagher entourage. Rory's unofficial bodyguard, he travelled everywhere with him. Indeed, it was Tom O'Driscoll who carried Rory's cherished Fender Stratocaster into the church in Wilton at Rory's funeral mass in June 1995.

Donal felt that Rory could only venture backstage if Tom went with him. Rory thought: 'I wasn't too afraid of Jerry Lee because I had worked on the sessions with him, but everybody else was obviously very scared because there was nobody else in the dressing room when Tom and I went in.' Rory proceeded to coax Jerry Lee out of his sulk with his unique charm and skills of diplomacy. 'We actually got to the point where we were just chatting away, reminiscing about the sessions and that kind of thing. All of a sudden the door opened and in walked John Lennon. There was a deathly silence for a couple of seconds. I just stared at Jerry Lee to see how he was going to react. Tom O'Driscoll couldn't resist this opportunity, he was a huge Beatles fan and he just went over to Lennon, dropped down on his knees, kissed his hand and said, "I've been waiting twenty years to get the autograph of the king of rock and roll."

'Of course, this drove Jerry Lee completely wild, he went for his sock, thinking he had a gun in it and then he started looking around for something to throw or break. Lennon could see all this, so he quickly signed Tom's piece of paper and then to defuse the situation, he took the pen and another piece of paper from Tom and went across the room to Jerry Lee. He did exactly what Tom had done to him, he went down on his knees, kissed Jerry Lee's hand and said "I've been waiting twenty years to get the autograph of the real king of rock and roll!" Jerry Lee was delighted, he signed the scrap of paper and they started talking and then everything was fine. It was a wonderful moment.'

Above and over: Checking the tuning while playing away. Rory is photographed in his home town by fellow Cork man Fin Costello. (© Fin Costello)

15
Irish
Tour
'74

J ANUARY 1974 found Rory Gallagher and his band touring Ireland again. It was the classic line-up of Lou Martin from Belfast on keyboards, Gerry McAvoy on bass, Rod De'Ath on drums, and Rory on guitars, vocals, and harmonica. They were joined by a film crew led by Tony Palmer. Palmer, who had first caught the power of Rory Gallagher when Taste played support at the Cream farewell concert in 1968, which he had filmed for television, originally intended to shoot just footage for a TV show; but as the tour progressed he developed the idea into a full-length feature film of Rory on tour. The album and the accompanying film features tracks from live performances in the Ulster Hall in Belfast, the Carlton Cinema in Dublin's O'Connell Street, and, naturally, Cork's City Hall.

Tony Palmer was a founding presenter of BBC Radio 4's *Kaleidoscope* arts programme. A former music critic for *The Observer*, he went on to become a prolific and distinguished film-maker. His groundbreaking *All You Need Is Love*, a seventeen-part series for television on American popular music, won several awards, as did his film *Wagner*, which starred Richard Burton alongside Laurence Olivier, John Gielgud, and Vanessa Redgrave. He also made a number of other rock documentaries, including *Rope Ladder to the Moon* with Cream bassist Jack Bruce (1969), *200 Motels* with Frank Zappa (1971), and *Bird on a Wire* with Leonard Cohen (1972).

Irish Tour '74, with its distinctive silver gatefold sleeve, was a natural successor to the highly successful *Live in Europe*. This time around, Rory and the band are introduced by Mickey Connolly, head of security for concert promoter Jim Aiken. Rory can be heard tuning in to 'Cradle Rock', written by Rory and taken from the *Tattoo* album that followed hot on the heels of *Blueprint*. Both Mickey Connolly and Jim Aiken had known Rory since his earliest days with Taste playing the Maritime in Belfast and were firm friends of the Gallagher family over several decades of touring in Ireland.

There are three cover versions on this album, starting with the second track, 'I Wonder Who', written by Rory's hero Muddy Waters. This song was a Chicago blues standard, no doubt sourced by Rory from the classic 1961 album by Ray Charles *The Genius Sings the Blues*. This was Charles' last album for Atlantic Records. It also featured Hank Snow's 'I'm Moving On', recorded by Rory in his days with Taste.

John Woods, Managing Director of Polydor (Ireland), one of the founding fathers of the Irish record industry, presents a platinum disc to Rory for sales in excess of 50,000 copies of *Irish Tour '74*. Gerry McAvoy (*centre*), Rod De'Ath (*second from right*) and Lou Martin (*right*) are also present on 10 June 1974 in the Savoy Cinema during the Cork Film Festival (courtesy *Irish Examiner* Publications).

The anthemic 'Tattoo'd Lady', a constant in Rory's live repertoire, follows 'I Wonder Who'. Rory then moves effortlessly to a J. B. Hutto classic which reflects the empathy between Rory and his devotees, where, like all teenagers, they know every word of their hero's material counting along with Rory on 'Too Much Alcohol' from ninety to one hundred.

The composer of 'Too Much Alcohol', one Joseph Benjamin Hutto, was born on 26 April 1926 in Blackville, Barnwell County, South Carolina. His father, Calvin, was a deacon. The family moved to Augusta, Georgia, in 1929 and J. B. began singing with the family group, The Golden Crowns Gospel Singers. A self-taught musician he moved to Chicago in the early 1940s and worked outside music while mastering drums, guitar, and piano. By the mid-1940s, he joined forces with Johnny Ferguson and the Twisters, subsequently forming his own outfit The Hawks, playing the 1015 Club, Globetrotter Lounge, and Sylvio's. Hutto was heavily influenced by Elmore James, Muddy Waters, and Texan bluesmeister Aaron Thibodeaux 'T-Bone' Walker. J.B. and The Hawks recorded widely in and around Chicago for Vanguard and Delmark and toured Europe on many occasions. J. B. passed away on 12 June 1983 in Harvey, Illinois. 'Too Much Alcohol' featured for many years in Rory's set list.

One of the most memorable images in Tony Palmer's film is the power of Rory's rendering of Tony Joe White's 'As The Crow Flies'.

White, the composer of 'Polk Salad Annie' and 'Rainy Night in Georgia', is the undisputed master of Swamp Blues. White also wrote 'Steamy Windows', recorded by Tina Turner. Rory had met up with Tony Joe at the Isle of Wight Festival in 1970. He performs this version of 'As the Crow Flies' on his 1932 National Steel Guitar.

Tony Joe White was born in Louisiana, the son of a cotton farmer. I spoke to him a few years ago when he was touring here for the late promoter Derek Nally. 'I've always been lucky with my writing, even at the very start with "Rainy Night in Georgia" and "Polk Salad Annie" and in my life doing the songs and the music that I wanted to and not depending on a record company or someone to say do this or that.

'We lived on a cotton farm down in Louisiana, on the river. We didn't have a whole lot! I had five sisters and my mum and dad and my older brother and they all played guitar and piano so we always had music. Then when we did get a turntable my brother brought home an album by Lightnin' Hopkins. I was about fifteen and I started leanin' into the guitar. I never listened to much country music growing up, I stayed with Lightnin' Hopkins, John Lee Hooker and Muddy Waters.

'It would be real hard for me to pick a personal favourite, but I do remember the first time I heard Brook Benton sing "Rainy Night in Georgia". The way he sang it was the way I wrote it. When I first heard it I played it back over fifty times in a row, it was just beautiful.'

Tony Joe remembered Rory. 'I'm real familiar with Rory's treatment of "As the Crow Flies". I've always really liked his singing and playing and have quite a few albums of his ... A real sweet man, I loved his playin'.'

"As The Crow Flies" is followed by yet another offering from *Tattoo*, this time the unforgettable Gallagher classic 'A Million Miles Away', where the audience of loyal fans play the role of call and response at the Belfast show in the Ulster Hall, which was in an area known locally at the time as 'Bomb Alley'. The audience of young men and women came from all over Northern Ireland for their fix of Rory's blistering playing. He was one of the few rock artists to play the province of Ulster during those turbulent times. Many of the audience were moved to tears from when the first chord struck, not just by the band's presence but by the passion of Rory's playing and his enthusiasm.

Donal Gallagher remembers the genesis of the song. 'I took Rory down to Ballycotton. He went off to the cliff and disappeared for a couple of hours. I was sitting waiting by the car when he came back. "Where have you been for the last few hours?" I said. "I had a great idea," Rory replied, "I got a song here today. I was a million miles away!!!"

'Walk On Hot Coals' has an almost jazz-like construction with the early pyrotechnics of Rory on guitar leading to each member of the band taking a solo and returning to the distinctive riff set by Rory on the Stratocaster. The album was warmly received because it was probably the best to date to capture the energy of his live playing.

The Irish premier of Tony Palmer's film was held in the Capitol Cineplex on Cork's Grand Parade as part of the Cork Film Festival. Rory and the band were in attendance.

Close ups of Rory's Stratocaster guitar – set those controls for the heart of the sun.

Rory in classic pose, on stage at the Lonestar Café in New York City (© Charlie Gili).

I F YOU LOOK REALLY CLOSELY at the after show party in the closing minutes of the *Irish Tour '74* film you just might spot its director Tony Palmer as he admits to 'joining in' on the Leadbelly classic 'Goodnight Irene'. He appears while Rory tries to encourage Tom O'Driscoll to join in the singing, and just before Mick Daly of The Lee Valley String Band comes into shot. I spoke to Tony recently about how he came to film Rory and where he first saw the guitarist.

Palmer first saw Rory play with Taste at the Cream farewell concert in 1968 at the Royal Albert Hall, which he filmed. 'I was very impressed with Taste. In fact after the first set – there were two shows that day – I went and complained to Robert Stigwood, saying don't you think that we should record them [Taste] as well. No, he said, so unfortunately we didn't film it.

'But I was very impressed by the band and woke up to Rory Gallagher's presence as it were and then began to follow him. Quite out of the blue, in the summer of 1973, his brother Donal approached me and said Rory was going on this tour and would I be interested in making a film. I said absolutely, of course. So although by then I had left the BBC I still had good contacts and went back to *Omnibus*, which was then the main arts programme on television. I suggested a programme on Rory and they said yes please so that's how the project was initiated.'

The sheer size and weight of some of the cameras and equipment of the time meant thought was required. 'When it came to talking and discussing the plans with Donal, Rory was very involved … We decided to shoot on 16 millimetre, which is also quite difficult – you need a lot of light so you can film because it's very slow negative stock. I said I could probably shoot it with two or three cameras, but you'd end up complaining that all these cameras were in the way … so I'm going to do it on one camera and I'll tell you where the camera is. I'm going to need a lot of light to see you properly and please don't wander off to the back of the stage out of light otherwise we're up shit creek without a paddle.

'To be fair, I don't think Donal or Rory were quite sure what I was saying, but as you know Rory was so unbelievably professional that he did get the point and that's why I got such wonderful shots of him playing, because he knew where the camera was … and I'm standing looking grumpy right behind it … so he always performed for the audience and for the one camera that was there. From a technical point of view, it was very primitive, but in a strange way that gives it its special atmosphere, I think.

'I think if we did it today … it would have sixteen mini-video cameras whizzing up and down … the silly thing on the crane that shoots across the audience and fast cutting and all that stuff.

'I had a long discussion with Bill Wyman about the Stones film by Scorcese "You Light Up My Arse…"!! Bill, of course, is not in it. Bill and I both agreed that the one thing it had was every conceivable facility. Scorcese said it had eighteen cameras. Charlie Watts told Bill there were twenty-five cameras. However many cameras they had, in the end what you miss is the real visceral excitement of going to a Stones concert. So that's today.'

In early 1975, following the departure of guitarist Mick Taylor, Rory actually had the chance to join the Rolling Stones. Rory's brother and manager Donal Gallagher received a call from the Rolling Stones management offices wondering if Rory might be interested because Mick Jagger saw a lot in him. The auditions were scheduled for The Hague and Rory travelled on his own, a fact that Donal, many years later, said he regretted. He was put up in a nearby hotel and jammed with the band at a nearby venue. Rory had a tour of Japan fast approaching and with no word from the Stones management packed his bags, leaving a note at the reception desk in the hotel: 'If you still want me, then I will hear from you.' Rory departed for Japan.

'Going back to 1974,' Tony Palmer continued, 'the limitations of the technology at our disposal in an odd way gave it the sort of excitement that I'm not sure that if we'd had so called better equipment that it would have helped us.

'In terms of Belfast I don't need to remind you of the kinds of problems that were going on at that time. Still, Rory insisted that he wanted to go there. I said "Oh, are you making a political statement." He laughed and said he wouldn't know a political statement if he saw it, but in the back of his mind it was very important for him … that he was seen to perform. That was a noble ambition and that's what we did.

'Going to Belfast I pointed out to him would be somewhat tricky for us, as the BBC Film Unit would insist that I inform them and they would inform Special Branch – and sure enough when we got to Belfast Airport we were met by two or three guys. They were terribly nice, plain clothes as it were, jeans and open neck shirts. One of them came up to me and said "I'm from Special Branch. I want you to know we'll make sure that you're ok." When we got to the Ulster Hall we were vaguely expecting trouble and these guys, the Special Branch, were there but in the end there was no trouble, Rory carried the audience along with him. Even he, Rory, was marginally apprehensive that there might be some sort of trouble. All kinds of things were rumoured. Everything went off very smoothly, there was no trouble at all, but it did give the actual concert a slight frisson.

'I remember when Rory and I talked about it later, when we went down to Cork in fact, that he said "How did you feel in the Ulster Hall?" I said that "I was with you, and I knew that you'd protect me Rory". He just laughed and thought it was very funny.

'Rory's talent was for a long time underestimated, I felt. That was why I wanted to make the film – he was a wonderful musician and I also liked the fact that there was absolutely no bullshit about him and absolute tunnel vision – very professional, minded very much that we reflected that in the film, very private man and wasn't too keen being filmed coming out of his mum's house [then in Sydney Park in Cork] but I said unless I put up a caption saying "This is your mother's house", nobody's going to know – that's the kind of person you are and I don't want to portray you as something that you are not.

'For me the most important thing was the music and I convinced him of that, and when he saw the cut of the film he just looked at me and he actually very gently took my wrist and said you kept your promise.

Rory and his beloved mother, Monica (Mona), at the then family home in Sydney Park, Cork, in the early 1970s (courtesy Gordon Morris).

'I hesitate to say this but I'm just a groupie. I'm in awe of these performers. I can't play any musical instrument myself so to some extent at that period of my career, even now with classical music, the people I make films about are people I'm in awe of ... this is the kind of genius I want to celebrate, I wanted people to know how good these people are ... We filmed Hendrix a few years before. I think I was the first ever person to film Hendrix and I'm often asked why did you film Jimi Hendrix – because I'd never heard anybody play the guitar like that before, why did you film Eric Clapton and Cream – because I'd never heard musicians play as well as that before. Lennon and McCartney I liked because they were songwriters of genius. Instrumentally they weren't that good. The great instrumental soloists such as Rory, these were people whose skill I was just in awe of and when that was coupled with considerable musicianship – every night. I think we filmed every concert on that tour and they were never the same and it was one of my big regrets that the film is only an hour and a bit long ... I wished it could have been much longer so you could have seen whole numbers or two versions of the same song and see how much he changes it each night.

'You never knew quite what he was going to do ... that's what made it very exciting and that's what the audience responded to too.

'I said to Rory once, a good while after we made *Irish Tour*, "I went to a Bob Dylan concert" and he said "How was it?" and I said "He kept reminding me of you." "How's that?" he enquired. I said: "He never said anything; he just got on and played". Rory enjoyed that. Rory got the audience with him because of what he did, what he played and not what he said ... it was through the music that Rory wished to speak and it was wonderful music making.

'By 1974, I had toured with Cream and with The Who so I was familiar with backstage facilities, which in those days were non existent. Today, a pipsqueak first-time pop outfit wouldn't tolerate what was being offered back then. That really makes me angry – what's that dreadful Canadian singer called ... yes Celine Dion ... she won't even agree to play in a venue unless there's a fluffy white carpet and her dressing room is covered in white lilies ... come on ... you couldn't sing your way out of paper bag dear.

'People often say to me how did you get such access, but it wasn't that I got access, there were simply no PR people, no record executives, no bouncers backstage stopping people coming back other than the obvious security. That was the same when we were on tour with Rory. Donal was there, of course, and promoter Jim Aiken but you weren't aware of swarms of overfed, overpaid nonentities PR people or even more dreadful moronic half-witted record executives … they just weren't there.

'I don't remember anyone wearing a backstage pass during Rory's tour, I really don't. But it wasn't as if it was open house, Donal, in particular, was careful in not letting the swarms come backstage. I don't think Rory would have worried. He would have worried beforehand because that's a period of intense concentration and preparing himself really. Rory was very disciplined: I admired that about him, I learnt that very early on. I'd known that from other very great musicians I'd been backstage with that the worst thing you can do before a concert is talk to them: they don't want to talk they're focused on what they are about to do.'

A large crowd enjoys Rory's set in fine sunshine in the grounds of Macroom Castle, County Cork, during the Macroom Mountain Dew Festival, Sunday 26 June 1977.

The ticket (left) is for the 1977 concert, the ticket (far left) is for the following year.

N JUNE 1977 the town of Macroom in County Cork hosted Ireland's first ever open air rock concert. It was part of the Macroom Mountain Dew Festival, and headlined by Rory Gallagher and his band. An audience of over three thousand people attended, not much compared to today's mass audiences, but a really important moment in the story of popular culture and music in Ireland. The festival also served as the launching pad for the just established *Hot Press*, an undertaking supported and encouraged in no small way by Rory and his brother Donal. The festival provided the magazine with its first cover – Rory – and with the energy that helped it take off.

This poster for the 'first ever major Irish rock festival' has Rory and his band as headliners for the open air concert in Macroom, County Cork, in June 1977. His Belgian pal Roland van Campenhout from Ghent was also on the bill.

Hot Press was founded by Niall Stokes. The first issue was released on 9 June 1977, a couple of weeks before the festival in Macroom. Priced at twenty pence, its contributors included Julian Vignoles, a major Rory Gallagher fan later to distinguish himself in broadcasting in both radio and television with RTÉ, Niall's brother Dermot, Oliver Sweeney covering traditional music, future film-maker Neil Jordan on the upcoming general election, distinguished writer Desmond Hogan at the Santa Cruz Poetry Festival, B. P. Fallon, ace publicist and rock fan, Brian Masterson on audio equipment, and Ross Fitzsimons. Photographic duties were handled by Jonathan Hession and Joe Jackson, with graphics by T. P. McCurtain, Larry Bennett, and Willie Finney.

The first issue celebrated Rory's forthcoming appearance at the festival in the grounds of Macroom Castle later that month. It also covered the Dublin Folk Festival that was due in July and the Dalymount Park gig on Sunday 21 August with Thin Lizzy headlining a bill that featured Graham Parker and the Rumour, Fairport Convention, and the emerging Boomtown Rats. *Hot Press* had their offices in 21 Upper Mount Street at the very top of several flights of stairs.

'The name only came after an inordinate amount of deliberation during which we must have gone through another thousand possibilities,' wrote Niall Stokes in his opening editorial. 'We thought at one stage of printing a list of the names we didn't pick, but we decided it would take too much space and besides we might want them again getting other projects off the ground. But if you're really stuck for a name for a band, why not drop in ...?'

'So what've we got to offer?' Niall continued. 'At this stage we'd better let the first issue speak for itself – it will anyway. But it is a beginning, a first move. We'd like to know how you feel about where we should go from here as well. No joke ... If the paper is good it'll inspire your interest and reaction and that's the size of it. We're confident that's the way it's going to turn out. For those who haven't been picking up on our publicity, we'll be producing *Hot Press* on a fortnightly basis so watch out for the paper again on the news stands in about thirteen days time. Buy it and keep buying it. Or why not subscribe?'

Hot Press survives to this day, despite several close run calls throughout the late 1970s and in the mid-1980s. It got through with the support not only of loyal readers but from musicians and industry bodies. In 1982, for example, Derek Nally promoted the fifth *Hot Press* Birthday Party gig 'A Day at the Races' in Punchestown Racecourse outside Dublin. The bill featured Rory Gallagher and his band, Bono, The Edge and Friends, Paul Brady, Simple Minds, De Danann and other special guests.

Dermot Stokes, Niall's brother and a regular contributor to the magazine in its early days, has always been a serious bluesman. I remember seeing him play piano with Blueshouse alongside Ed Deane in Slattery's of Capel Street on a Sunday afternoon in the late 1960s, those exciting blues performances that sent us home on the bus eager to discover more of the roots of this music and chewing on a packet of Silvermints to disguise the fumes of several pints of Smithwicks shandy. Slattery's was the spiritual home of African-American blues music in Dublin of the 1960s, with Eddie Soye, John Sawyer, Ray Astbury, and Larry Roddy ensuring that we got to hear and see some of the surviving pioneers of this musical form like Mississippi Fred McDowell and Champion Jack Dupree.

One album that Dermot remembers from that period was titled *Mississippi Blues*. 'It was a compilation of field recordings that were made with a couple of guys just wandering around the Mississippi area. They were picking up all these people who were doing variations of Muddy Water's tunes, of Robert Johnson stuff, Son House and these inevitably were all influences! I remember buying that in Murray's

Philip Lynott (left), Rory (centre) and Paul Brady (right) on stage for the *Hot Press* 5th Birthday Bash at Punchestown Racecourse in 1982. The event was promoted by the late Derek Nally. (© Colm Henry)

down on the quays. It opened another gate into Mississippi blues, into listening to people like Robert Johnson, whom I would have a huge interest in and an artist I would take down from the shelf again and again, and as you say – Charley Patton, people like that, shouting Mississippi blues.'

At that time, there were very few places where you could find out about this form of music. It was entirely underground, through word of mouth, like a secret society. Dermot remembers going into Murray's and looking for Louis Jordan music and being told rather forlornly by George Murray that (a) they couldn't get it and (b) when they did, it was always gone within moments.

The first time Dermot saw Rory play was in Stella House in Mount Merrion when he was still with Taste. 'I thought the Stella gig was a great gig. What was really interesting about it was that, apart altogether from the energy and the skill and the power of it, it didn't pay lip service to the kind of "chart" thing which pretty much all beat groups had to do at that time.

'There were a lot of very fine musicians playing around Dublin, fantastic music, soul-based music, but at the same time there was always a sense that people had to acknowledge what was happening in the charts and that was one thing you could say for sure that Taste did not do, they just went out and did their thing.'

Dermot Stokes remembers speaking with Donal and Rory in the late 1970s about the challenges of touring whilst writing an 'On the Road' special for the fledgling *Hot Press*. 'We hooked up in London at Tom O'Driscoll's house and travelled by truck with the gear across to Belgium and Germany and so on. Rory was rooted in the way Europe worked long before we were so conscious of being Europeans, he knew how Europe worked and, in fact, based himself in Ghent in Belgium for a year in the early 1970s, because he had to connect. People forget how difficult it was to travel to gigs in those rather primitive days of air travel. Now you turn up at an airport and get on a flight and your truck goes to the venue.'

'In those days,' Dermot recalls, 'it was … it was into the truck and bouncing along in the truck. I have to say, early on, Rory and his brother and manager Donal became quite adept at organising transport by plane where they possibly could. At one point, Donal and Rory hired a guy (Peter Collins) that used to be a travel agent to come in and be part of the team, and much of their history as an outfit involves flying in various crates of varying descriptions, pioneers in the style of Amelia Earhart.

'I think that the hugely important thing that Rory did early on in his career was to establish that an Irish band could form itself, could play original material, could do it here in Ireland first of all, and could then take it to London, could make it in London, then take it to Europe and make it in Europe and then take it around the world. In many respects, Taste, first of all, and then Rory were the first bands to do that from this country. That's the fundamental example that they set.'

In terms of Rory's recordings, Dermot felt it was hard to choose which album in particular stands out. He would prefer to go for individual tracks, 'say 'Philby' as the first one. I remember discussing it with him. He used electric sitar on it which he'd hired from Pete Townshend. One of the striking things about Rory, apart altogether from the legacy which he left and the example which he gave, which I think was enormous, is who he was as a songwriter, as a character. Very early on he was writing his own music. He was funnelling a lot of influences into the music and it came out as quite clearly – Rory.

'This evolved over time and he began to assume a character. That character was essentially a loner, this person arriving in town to usually a fairly dark and bleak landscape, it's kind of a "film noir" landscape, and where there are characters who are threatening or, in some way, dark influences. You find in some of his lyrics that Rory is like a Raymond Chandler character or a Laurence Block, a character from one of those novels which he consumed in huge quantities. He just loved that kind of American detective, hard-boiled fiction and you'll hear town hall and the mayor and all those characters and situations in his music.

'The American version is the guy in a trench coat. A stranger comes in with a monkey on his back and a problem that he has got to solve. In the European context it's more about spies and espionage, the same thing with a slightly hunted type of character. I've often wondered about Rory, the times I would have met him, talking to him about what he was writing and why he was working in this way. It often seemed to me that there was some element of dislocation for him, that he felt slightly dislocated from where he was and that he identified in a very strong way with the Philby's, the spies, the people kicking around cities in the dark, in America or Europe. That, of course, is in many ways the life of an itinerant musician, you arrive in a city, you go to the venue, you do your sound check, you go to your hotel room – and for somebody who worked as hard as Rory and gigged as often and as relentlessly as Rory, increasingly he must have felt that there were comparatively few places that he had the "root" if you like. He was always like those spies or detectives, Pinkerton men, or whatever it was, the loner coming through without making a huge impression on the water as they passed through.'

18
Joe O'Herlihy

While unloading the band's gear in Dayton, Ohio, in July 1976, Tom O'Driscoll carries the treasured VOX amplifier, flanked by 'Spooner' (left) and Joe O'Herlihy. (© Fin Costello).

A VITAL PRESENCE on Rory Gallagher's tours in the mid- to late-1970s was soundman Joe O'Herlihy. Born in Cork, O'Herlihy would go on to become one of the most sought after soundmen in the world, working for many years with the all-conquering U2. 'The first time I came across Rory's music was in mid-1968,' Joe told me recently, 'just after his first single, "Blister on the Moon", came out on the Major Minor Label. Some of my mates, Gerry Walsh and Leo Bailey, were big into music and were raving about this record by a young Cork bloke.

'I was hooked first and foremost as a fan, so when the *Taste* and *On The Boards* albums came out, we immediately bought them and spent months religiously listening to them, all the while looking forward to going to the Rory shows at Christmas time, when he would come back home to Ireland on his short Irish tours. Between 1968 and 1971, I saw Rory play a half a dozen times, including his legendary appearance at the Isle of Wight Festival in August 1970. If you listen carefully to the live recordings from that show, I am sure you can hear me screaming from the front row "Come on Rory boy". In early 1971, Rory formed his own band, The Rory Gallagher Band, and as per normal he returned home at Christmas time for his customary Irish tour. By then, I was working with a local band Chapter Five and they got the support slot for the Cork gig. So began my annual association with Rory's homecoming gig where local bands like Chapter Five, Gaslight, and Sleepy Hollow provided the support through '71, '72, '73, '74, '75. Year in year out, I'd meet up with Donal Gallagher and Tom O'Driscoll for these gigs and really got to know and like them, and I felt the feeling was mutual.

'From the early to mid-1970s, I had a real job working in Crowley's Music Centre, first on Merchants Quay and then on to MacCurtain Street after we moved there. When Rory was at home in Cork he would always just drop in to say hello and chat to us about his gigs and tours around the world. The late Mick Crowley always loved to see Rory, and every time Rory came into the shop, Mick would always enquire about the already famous, and now legendary, Strat that Rory bought in the shop, just a few years previously.

'During the filming of Rory's documentary *Irish Tour '74*, there is a scene shot in Crowley's Music Centre, where you can see me handing Rory a new Martin D35 acoustic guitar. That was probably when Rory first met me and knew who I was. At the time, I was also working with Sleepy Hollow, who supported Rory on the *Irish Tour '74* dates. Donal Gallagher arranged for Sleepy Hollow to do a UK College Tour supporting Rory for about six weeks through May, June '75, that's when I got my first real taste of the touring life, six weeks of bliss.

'Later in 1975, Sleepy Hollow were again asked to support Rory for his annual Christmas shows. It was during this tour that Donal Gallagher offered me the opportunity to work for Rory on a permanent basis. Boy, what a Christmas present. Twenty-one years old, brand new passport in hand, US visa acquired, I arrived in Chicago in early January 1976. My first gig with Rory was at the Uptown Theatre in Milwaukee, Wisconsin, on the freezing shores of Lake Michigan, sharing the bill with Jim Dandy's Black Oak Arkansas.

'It was minus twenty degrees outside, the coldest I had ever experienced. Tom O'Driscoll gave one look at me and said with a chuckle in his beautiful west Cork brogue, "Wait until we get to Minnesota. You'll love it there," and so my rapid and steep learning curve began. The rest of 1976 was spent touring the USA, Europe and the UK. We even toured behind the Iron Curtain in Poland, which was a nerve-wracking experience back then. Then it was into Musicland Studios in Munich to record *Calling Card*, after that it was back to the USA to continue touring.

'During '76 we got to share the stage with some fantastic bands and artists, for example, Black Oak Arkansas, Hall & Oates, Ted Nugent, Kansas, Jethro Tull, Robin Trower, Dave Mason, Rick Derringer, Aerosmith, Blue Oyster Cult, ELO, Camel, Bachman Turner Overdrive, Canned Heat, and The Doobie Brothers. We even got to play at two festivals in the one day on 28 August 1976, The Rottweil Festival in Germany, then back to the UK to headline the Reading Rock Festival. All in a day's work, a million miles away from the Cork Boat Club on a Friday night with Sleepy Hollow. Bob Dylan showed up to meet Rory when we played at the Shrine auditorium in LA and we were special guests with ZZ Top on their "World Wide Texas Tour", a great few shows with a very big production. Then, as per normal, it was home for the Christmas and New Year Irish Tour, a chance to catch my breath and pinch myself, wondering what just happened.

'1977 started the same way as the previous year with a heavy touring schedule planned through January, February, March, April around the UK and Europe, and then it was into the summer festival season. The standout gig of the summer of '77 for me was the first

Irish rock festival on 26 June at the first Macroom Mountain Dew Festival. A European tour was next and that went on through August, September, and October. After that it was off to Japan from the middle of October through 6 November. Then after that Japanese tour we headed into the studio to record a new album.

'We arrived in San Francisco in early November for a projected six weeks of recording at His Masters Wheels recording studio with Elliott Mazer as producer. We worked right up to Christmas, when we all got to go home for a break. The plan was to return to San Francisco in early January 1978. Despite everything appearing to go well, there was an unspoken sense of unease before we all left to go home. I put it all down to the fact that it was a very tall order making this record after completing a year and a half of hard slog on a world tour.

'We returned to San Francisco in early January to finish mixing the album. While there, Rory went to see The Sex Pistols perform at the Winterland Ballroom. That gig made a huge and lasting impression on him. The energy of Punk was the driving force behind his eagerness to get back to basics, the rawness of guitar, bass, and drums was something Rory had realised he missed and longed to get back to. With the album completed, mixing and mastering done, or so we thought, we learned that Rory was not at all happy with the finished product. What happened next was like a complete bolt from the blue. He announced that he was canning the album, breaking up the band, and going to start a fresh new approach with a new band and would record the album all over again but this time in Europe. To make things worse, Rory had an accident with a car door while in LA rendering him out of action with a broken thumb for six weeks.

'Fulfilling contractual commitments for European dates and a UK tour, the Rory Gallagher Band mark 2 finished up the end of April. These were the last gigs with Rod De'Ath and Lou Martin. Gerry McAvoy would continue on bass in the new Rory Gallagher Band mark 3, joined by Ted McKenna, a power house rock solid drummer in the mould of John Bonham.

'With this new, slimmed down line-up we set about a summer of European rock festivals, including another trip to the Macroom Castle Rock Festival for some more mountain dew. There were also three shows with Bob Marley and the Wailers in Scandinavia, at Roskilde, Hortens, and Helsinki on 1, 2 and 3 July.

'Then some unfinished business – we went to Dieter Dierks Recording Studios in Cologne, Germany, in July and August to rerecord the album, which eventually became *Photo-Finish* and was released in October 1978. More UK and European dates followed, starting in September. The Glasgow Apollo Theatre was my last show and I finished working for Rory on 8 September 1978.'

'I felt that I graduated with an honours degree from the Rory Gallagher University of Rock and Roll,' Joe told me, 'and, to put it mildly, I have spent the last thirty-odd years working on my Master's doctorate. Rory gave me the ultimate rock and roll apprenticeship, not to mention a grounding in life matters, human awareness, and responsibilities, things that have followed me right through my life so far.'

Rory in full
flight at
The Venue,
London,
in 1980
(© Fin
Costello).

110

THE MID- TO LATE 1970s were a prolific time for Rory, releasing four well-received albums in five years: *Against the Grain* (1975), *Calling Card* (1976), *Photo-Finish* (1978) and *Top Priority* (1979).

Another highlight from the period was Rory's appearance on the first Rockpalast music special on German television in the summer of 1977, a remarkable show that brought the young Cork musician into millions of living rooms all over Europe. Rory had been something of a regular on early pop shows in Germany, going back even to his days with Taste. Although by 1977 he was with a new record company, Chrysalis, it helped that Rory had been signed to Polydor, a record label with German headquarters, for so long.

Peter Ruchel and Christian Wagner of Westdeutscher Rundfunk (WDR) television station had worked with Rory from the early 1970s. When planning the first Rockpalast special, they called Donal to check the guitarist's availability. While Rory was scheduled to appear on stage at Montreux Jazz Festival the night before the televised special, Donal confirmed his brother's appearance on the show, which was also to feature Little Feat and Roger McGuinn of the Byrds.

The occasion for the Rockpalast was to act as a link between the station's normal closing time of midnight and the beginning of coverage of a Muhammad Ali versus Earnie Shavers fight due for transmission at around four in the morning. WDR had, under the auspices of the European Broadcasting Union, granted member television networks the option to carry this historic broadcast throughout Europe.

'Kicking off the live broadcast at midnight, Rory and the band gave a tour de force performance to an audience of 50 million viewers,' wrote Donal in the sleeve notes to *Rory Gallagher – Shadow Play – The Rockpalast Concerts*. 'The show was a tremendous success and was

Many souvenir items were produced for Rory Gallagher, including pin badges (courtesy Gordon Morris) and books of matches.

beamed out via the Eurovision network (also on radio) covering the whole continent, reaching to countries within the Soviet Union/Iron Curtain at that time. Backstage, there was wonderful camaraderie between all the musicians, needless to say. Lowell George of Little Feat and Rory hit it off big time and, after some ten years, Roger McGuinn was reacquainted with Rory as he'd opened for the Byrds in London in 1966.

'Next came a Rockpalast show in Wiesbaden in 1979. Rory was already in Cologne and was recording the *Photo-Finish* album at Dieter Dierks Studio with new drummer Ted McKenna from Scotland, formerly of the Sensational Alex Harvey Band, and regular bassman Gerry McAvoy. The break from the studio was a welcome one and it felt like having the weekend off for Rory. Arriving in Wiesbaden the evening before for a press reception at the Buck Hotel – it seemed like a "local gig" with Frankie Miller on the bill as well. As usual, the backstage friendly atmosphere led to an inevitable "jam session".

'Rockpalast had become a televisual phenomenon with people hosting all night parties throughout Europe when a special was transmitted, line-ups included The Grateful Dead, The Who, Van Morrison, and Rick James.

'Being the first artist to play the show, Rory's name became synonymous with the Rockpalast series and, in 1982, another return appearance was demanded by fans of the show. This time, the setting was out of doors in Loreley, on the banks of the River Rhine. By now, Rory had changed and augmented his line-up again to include John Cooke on keyboards; Brendan O'Neill on drums; Gerry McAvoy on bass; with the twin saxes of Ray Beavis and Howie Casey extending the range and colour of the extended two hour plus set with Rory and the band returning later to jam with Eric Burdon, David Lindley, former King Crimson and Street Legal drummer Ian Wallace, and members of the German band Bap.'

Back in 1977, on the day before Rockpalast, Rory had played a set at the Montreux Jazz Festival on the shores of Lake Geneva. He appeared at the festival regularly throughout the 1970s. This festival, founded by Claude Nobs, has been lionised by Deep Purple in the rock classic 'Smoke on the Water'.

'In 1970,' Nobs recalls on the Montreux Collection DVD, 'I went to the Isle of Wight festival with a lot of cash (at least at that time) in my backpack to hopefully sign The Doors and Jimi Hendrix for

Rory checks out the machine head (© Fin Costello).

Bass man Gerry McAvoy, a native of Belfast and former member of Deep Joy, alongside Rory (courtesy Fin Costello).

rock shows I was producing in Montreux, but after I saw Taste with Rory Gallagher on stage, I decided to hire them too! I went back to Switzerland with agreements for the three groups and was very happy. Unfortunately, Jimi died before the scheduled performance and The Doors cancelled their European tour. But I still had Taste and hired Cactus to play on the same night. My friendship with Rory was immediate as we both love the blues and he came back with his own group to play at the Montreux Jazz Festival at least five times. Rory was one of the nicest people I ever met, as quiet backstage as he was wild on stage. The day he died I knew that rock and blues in Montreux would never be the same.'

Rory checks his mandolin backstage at the Ulster Hall in Belfast in 1979. Fin Costello took this photograph as Chris Welch interviewed Rory for *Melody Maker* (© Fin Costello).

ALTHOUGH BEST KNOWN for his electric playing, Rory Gallagher was also admired for his ability with the acoustic guitar. He spoke about this aspect to his career with Stefan Grossman in a 1978 issue of *Guitar Player*. 'With acoustic guitar, for the first couple of years at least, I think that you should leave a wound third string on and really build up strength in the fingers. In other words, don't try bending strings the first week you buy the guitar. Kids are lucky nowadays; you can get a Yamaha or something, and the cheaper model guitars are much better quality than they were years ago when you got this stuff with terrible action. The first guitar I got cost over four pounds, which was about twenty dollars then, in the good old days. After a while you get that urge to say: "To hell with this – I'm going to bend this string, instead of sliding up." But you have to build that up.

'If you're a kid with ears the size of the moon and an amazing sense of direction, who has heard Son House or Blind Boy Fuller or any of the National steel body players, then go ahead and buy the National, because that's a great place to start. The National I have, made in 1932 (purchased in the East Village in New York in the company of John Hammond), the neck joins the body at the twelfth fret, which is unfortunate. I prefer the fourteenth fret, but I can live with that. You just have to ride over the body with the slide. The action on it isn't bad, and the tuning is good. Obviously, it's loud and banjo-like, and there's only a certain amount of sustain in it, but I think that it slightly dictates what you play. For instance, you don't really bend strings much on a National; you use it more as a straightforward heavy-playing, ragtime guitar, or you play in the Son House bottleneck school.'

Asked by Grossman about his acoustic playing, Rory talked about his Martin guitar. 'I play a Martin D35. I use the National for things like "Pistol Slapper Blues", which I play faster than Blind Boy Fuller did, and a J. B. Hutto song called "Too Much Alcohol", which he plays electric, of course. There's always the nature of the banjo in the National, I find, and you have to play it sort of like that. I do anyway.'

On the Martin set up: 'At present I'm doing numbers like Leadbelly's "Out on the Western Plain", where the tuning is D, A, D, G, A, D (low to high). It's a D tuning, except that the G remains a G. "Out on the Western Plain" was always one of my schoolboy favourites, because of the lyrics. I thought, here's Leadbelly singing a song about cowboys, and it didn't seem to be a part of the black culture. But as it turns out, there were African-American cowboys. So I was fiddling around

Rory warms up his acoustic guitar in the Metropole Hotel on MacCurtain Street, Cork, on 3 January 1974 – spot the cords! (courtesy *Irish Examiner* Publications).

with slack D, or whatever they call it, and I found that there's instant unison. If you use a two fret interval on the second and third strings, you can go up like a dulcimer or a sitar. At any point up the neck, if you hit the second string at a certain fret and hit the third string two frets up, then those notes are the same. You get a kind of raga, dulcimer type of thing. So it seemed such a nice idea to do the Leadbelly song in that semi-Celtic-come-whatever style. It's never quite major or minor, so you can do tricks with it.'

Rory got his much cherished mandolin Martin OM (Orchestra Model) from Clifford Essex in late 1970 soon after Taste broke up. 'It was a beautiful round body thing. I started working on it then, but I didn't play it until I started in 1971 with the band. I moved from that to an electric mandola. Chris Eccleshall [who maintained, restored and built many of the guitarist's acoustic instruments in his workshop in Devon] made me an acoustic mandola and I used to play that with a pick up. I've been thinking of using that again recently. The difference in sound between the electric mandola and acoustic mandolin is fairly extreme for what we were doing.'

Throughout his career, Rory made no secret of his love of folk and traditional music, whatever its origins. In March 1984, he played a series of shows with renowned folk musicians Juan Martin, Richard Thompson and David Lindley. The concerts were the brainchild of Paul Charles, co-founder of the concert and booking agency Asgard. Paul was, in fact, one of the first managers of a rock band I met in the 1970s, when he was looking after northern rock group Fruup. Other rock band managers of the time were Morrison and O'Donnell taking care of Philip Lynott, Donal Gallagher handling Rory's affairs, and

Paul McGuinness who handled Irish trad rock sensation Spud. By the end of the decade, McGuinness was to manage U2; the rest is part of rock and roll history.

Rory's playing in the company of Lindley, Thompson, and Martin shone through on the tour; many in the audience were there to see the man in the checked shirt and were not disappointed. One of the tracks played – 'Flight to Paradise' written by Juan Martin and in a form of flamenco duel between the two guitarists – was to appear on the posthumously released album *Wheels Within Wheels*. In the sleeve notes to this album, Donal refers to the enthusiasm Rory had for both Martin Carthy's playing and also for Bert Jansch. 'Another favourite of Rory's was Bert Jansch. My encounter with Bert was a year after Rory's passing. When we met up we talked of Rory's unfulfilled folk album. Bert said "Did you know that Rory and I did some things together?" The result was "She Moved Thro' the Fair/An Crann Ull". Also on that album you can hear 'Bratacha Dubha' (Black Flags) with Martin Carthy, Chris Newman, and Maire Ní Cathasaigh. Rory was a fan of Chris and Maire and, according to Donal, their gig at the Troubadour may well be one of the last Rory saw prior to his passing. Chris and Maire played at the memorial service for Rory in the Brompton Oratory in November 1995.

Colin Harper, in his wonderful biography of the late Bert Jansch and the British folk and blues revival *Dazzling Stranger*, writes that during the first half of 1994, 'Bert was often bumping into blues/rock guitar hero Rory Gallagher down at the Troubadour, which, along with Bunjies, was one of the few original folk venues in London still functioning. Rory, though ill, had been an admirer of Bert's music for years and was keen to involve both Bert and Martin Carthy in a planned acoustic album. He had got as far as sending demos to Bert, hoping to arrange a still more extraordinary collaboration: "He actually wanted to work with Anne Briggs," says Bert. "But she thought he was a pop star and rejected the idea out of hand. Then I suggested Maggie Boyle. Maggie lived in Yorkshire and came down to London especially to meet Rory and record the stuff that we'd arranged but he didn't show up. He just drew a blank, couldn't remember having arranged it."' However, in a letter to friend Gordon Morris in Cumbria in June 1994, Rory seemed very aware of his acoustic recording plans, so there may be something lost in translation.

21

A Sense of Ireland

Official programme for A Sense of Ireland, a groundbreaking festival in London that showcased the range of Irish arts, literature, music and culture.

N MARCH 1980, Rory Gallagher was one of the artists chosen to represent Ireland at the A Sense of Ireland festival in London. Playing at the Lyceum on the Strand under the heading of Rock and New Wave, Rory's performance was part of a wide-ranging programme reflecting the best of contemporary Irish music, theatre, literature, creative arts, and cinema – the arts in all its guises

The thinking behind the festival was much deeper than simply highlighting Irish talent, as the programme director John Stephenson made clear in the official programme, for this was a time when the Irish in Britain were looked upon very suspiciously, the bombings of the 1970s fresh in many minds.

'I grew up in London and Leeds under the shadow of the 1950s bombing campaign by the IRA,' Stephenson wrote. 'At some stage, every Irish immigrant in England has had the experience of being called "an Irish pig", and of being an object of fear, hate or derision at least indirectly but often personally. The tragedy of this situation is primarily England's. As a child I reacted with tears and fierce and floundering pride. The shame was my accuser's, but it drove me into myself. The Irish in Britain have internalised this kind of thing by retreating into various mental ghettoes across a spectrum from the chameleon to the strident "paddy", all of them artificial. Layers of disguise became our survival mechanism, but the warps thus created do us more harm. We define ourselves in reaction.

'The fear is mutual. There was the English couple who watched for weeks as their winter coal supply disappeared, rather than inform us that we were going to the wrong bunker. At least the fun of that emerged and they became friends, like so many others who were, and are, good friends. England's history has produced a people who are at once the most tolerant and intolerant. This world-wise people have developed two mutually contradictory views of the Irish, both of which they hold at any given time to be true. On the one hand we are lazy, primitive, drunken, stupid and violent. On the other we are witty, cultured, gregarious, charming and lovable. In this mythology we are limited to being oafish ogres or spritely elves. Even personal acquaintance doesn't totally eliminate the general myths, as they remain an underlying view among our English friends and colleagues which slip out in unguarded moments; and also sadly because too many of us resort to these myths ourselves.

'The name of this festival represents our aspiration that, by presenting a sense of what is happening today in the Arts in Ireland, we may help to make some sense to our English neighbours of what we are as a people.'

'A Sense of Ireland,' he concluded, 'spans the established and anti establishment, the new and uncertain, the great tradition, the funny and the serious, the quiet and the loud. It makes no great claims nor any apologies. It is true and representative. It is there.'

Stocktons Wing, the Chieftains, the Boomtown Rats and a young U2 were just a few of the other Irish acts to perform. The organiser of the rock series was the legendary Frank Murray, tour manager for Thin Lizzy and later to manage Shane MacGowan and the Pogues.

The traditional music section of A Sense of Ireland was organised by P. J. Curtis. Curtis, a producer, writer, and broadcaster of note, would get to work much more closely with Rory at the end of the decade.

P. J. told the Irish guitarist Barry McCabe about meeting up with Rory in Edinburgh while acting as tour manager for the Chieftains in 1988.

'We talked and I asked him if he would consider doing a session on a forthcoming Davy Spillane album, *Out of the Air*, I was planning to work on the following year. Rory was delighted to be asked and expressed real excitement at the prospect of working with uileann pipes and also working with Davy. I was equally excited that he should agree as I was a huge fan of Rory's, and was keen to hear the result of two such soulful players from different traditions coming together on record.

'Following my meeting with Rory, I kept in touch through Donal and discovered that Rory was to be in Dublin the very week that I was in Windmill Studios recording with Davy. It was then just a matter of asking him to come to the studio whenever he was free. He was thrilled that the session was on and he gave us a date.

'We did two tracks, "Litton Lane" [a well known band rehearsal venue and equipment hire company] and "One for Phil". There was very little rehearsal, just a few run-throughs to get tuning/balance/ feel ... I wanted a spontaneous energy to be generated from these two great musicians coming together for the first time.

'Rory knew all of Davy's stuff; he was particularly knocked out by the previous album *Atlantic Bridge* on Tara Records where Davy played with Albert Lee among others. The two tracks took no more than two or three hours (not including the sitting around talking guitars/blues/life and laughing) ... it was a very happy session and a lot of banter and jokes all around. I had a ball that day and I believe so did Rory, Davy and the entire band.

'The session took the form of some loose jamming and "One for Phil" was the second piece we recorded. I had in mind that perhaps they might attempt a Robert Johnson piece with just acoustic and pipes/whistle. Rory played Davy's guitar – a 1930s vintage Silvertone – and while they warmed up Rory repeated a riff, which I liked, and Davy blew some low whistle. I asked that they develop the theme and "One for Phil" was the result of a long one-take effort. Rory and Davy had been chatting about Phil Lynott who had not long since died and hence the title.

'As for "Litton Lane", I wanted a basic tough, hard driving twelve bar blues track, where the pipes might fill the space normally filled by blues harp (harmonica) ... "Litton Lane" was the result, after several runs to work out an arrangement, with Rory playing his acoustic slide intro on Davy's Silvertone, then switching to the Stratocaster on the pick up ... then it was every man for himself! I had to do a number of takes to get the one that had IT ... the spark of energy that would raise it above the normal twelve bar session. I recall Rory suggesting some licks to Davy who, as a traditional player, would not be too conversant with the language and framework of the blues.

'We talked for a good hour before the instruments were taken from their cases, we could have talked through the entire booked studio session ... talking about old blues records, blues players. I promised to make Rory a tape of old bluesmen slide players like Barbecue Bob. I was tickled pink when Rory told me that he had many of my RTÉ Radio 1 *House of R&B* radio programmes on cassette. He said he had them taped here in Ireland and sent to him in London and he played them constantly on the road. As it emerged Rory had listened to exactly the same stuff on 1950s radio as I had. We talked about the possibility of me doing some more work with him. I regret that it never came about. He knew traditional music well ... loved the uileann pipes, Seamus Ennis, Willie Clancy, and Paddy Keenan, felt the soul of it keenly. He had been knocked out that members of the Chieftains had come to see him play live.

'I felt so honoured and proud that I got the opportunity to work with such a musician ... and a personal idol of mine from the 1960s. I had seen him first play with Taste as support to Cream at the Cream Farewell Concert in the Royal Albert Hall in 1968, and many times after that with his various trio line-ups. He was one of the most exciting performers I have ever seen, a truly great player and singer ... he cared about music ... he cared about guitars ... he cared about his craft ... he cared ... period!'

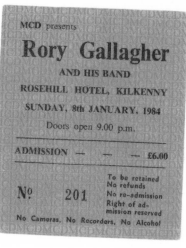

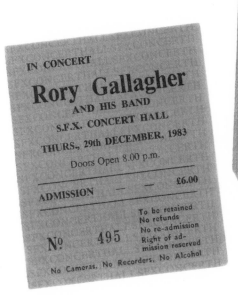

Marcus Connaughton speaking during one of his 'Rory Gallagher – A Walking Tour of Cork' events in Rory Gallagher Place at the entrance to Paul's Street Shopping Centre. The sculpture to the left of the photograph was unveiled on 25 October 1997 and was designed by Geraldine Creedon, a childhood friend of Rory's.

22

Rory looks for inspiration in New York (© Charlie Gili).

*S**TAGESTRUCK* was released in 1980, followed two years later by *Jinx*. The latter album was recorded in Dieter Dierks Studios in Cologne in Germany, with former Brinsley Schwarz keyboard maestro Bob Andrews complemented by the saxophones of Ray Beavis and Dick Parry. Highlights from the album included 'The Devil made Me Do It', 'Big Guns', and 'Double Vision'. One of my favourites from the album has always been Rory's treatment of Louisiana Red's 'Ride On Red, Ride On', a portrait of the apartheid that existed south of the Mason-Dixon Line.

> We made it into Shreveport where we were supposed to eat
> I got myself a sandwich and ate it on the street
> Ride On, Louisiana Red, Ride On
> Gonna ride on to your freedom
> And make those Northern States your home
> (Composers; Levy/Glover/Reid)
> (Published by Planetary – Nom (Ldn) Ltd)

Nevertheless, the early 1980s were a difficult period for Rory. Rock and blues based artists took a back seat to punk. And magazines like *Melody Maker* that had lauded Rory were overtaken by the more anarchic *NME*.

Harry Shapiro, biographer of Eric Clapton and many other 1970s musical heroes, had this to say to me about the period.

'When punk hit in this country it wasn't only Rory that suffered ... Most – like Alvin Lee, guitar player with Ten Years After – they went to Europe, I mean that's where their audience was. They went and they were packing them out in Scandinavia, Germany, and Italy; in this country – forget it. And I think Rory Gallagher and a number of "like" people, their audiences just evaporated ... At that point, the whole kind of blues/rock thing, given the relatively small size of the English market, just goes, and Rory went with it.'

The albums may have dried up for a while, but Rory never stopped touring, with one hundred concerts in sixty-five cities in twelve countries in sixteen weeks de rigeur for the band. He still had Europe and a very strong following and fan base there, with fan clubs in Sweden, Switzerland, Germany, Holland, and elsewhere. 'We've always kept an eye on Europe, we've never starved it,' he said. 'You can't, audiences change every two years or so in Europe, if you're

Lisdoonvarna Festival poster for 30 and 31 July 1983. Rory headlined the Saturday night show. (courtesy Dino McGartland).

away too long you find a slight shift in your audience, if you are good enough – people still want to hear you, but you can easily lose touch with people who've grown up with you.'

It was an activity he never really saw as work. 'I don't need stimulants to play, the music itself is enough,' Rory told journalist Colm McGinty, then of the *Evening Herald*, prior to the Lisdoonvarna Festival in 1983. 'We're just back from doing a festival in Switzerland and a couple of gigs at the Marquee Club in London, so we're nicely battle hardened, well warmed up. Doing the Marquee was fun, it's the club's twenty-fifth anniversary and it was a long time since we were there before, the idea is that everyone who ever played the place over the years would do a show this year as part of the celebrations. The Police did a couple and The Who have promised a set. It's a great idea because through the years you never know who might turn up.'

Rory also spoke about being, in essence, a member of the Irish diaspora before returning to the subject of touring. 'I've been living in London now for well over ten years, I suppose. It's a working base, and I come over here [to Ireland] often enough not to feel committed to the place. I don't regard myself as a permanent exile or anything like that, but it's a great place to work in, a very creative city. And though I suppose Irish people have a love-hate relationship with London, it's a place where you can get your work done. Though, I suppose I could just as easily live in New York, Hamburg or Los Angeles,' he laughs. 'I'm quite used to moving around.

'We used to tour Britain more a few years ago, but now we seem to play abroad a lot more … that's not a policy, it's simply the way things worked out. I mean, some years it's crazy. We might do two months in the States, a month in Australia and Japan, then back across Europe and maybe into the studio to do an album.

'So there wouldn't be hardly any time off at all. In a year like that it doesn't really matter where you live. You aren't going to see home anyway,' he groans. 'But no, these days I do try to plan things a little

Rory backstage at the Ulster Hall in Belfast on 6 January 1979 preparing his instruments and bottlenecks for the show. Rory is talking to the journalist Chris Welch (off camera) who, along with Fin Costello, was covering that year's Irish Tour for *Melody Maker* magazine (© Fin Costello).

better. In the old days, we didn't plan anything, we were just like gypsies or nomads, it was one town, one country after another, all great fun, but you end up chasing your own tail.

'I see music as a lifetime affair,' Rory told McGinty. 'I'm not in it for the big kill and then get out. I hope to be playing strong when I'm fifty, like people I admire, your art improves with age. You see I love what I do, I don't treat it like a job of work; it's more a compulsive hobby. Even if I want to get away on holiday, I still end up packing a guitar and a tape recorder,' he laughs. 'We've toured the States twenty times now and we do better there than is commonly known, although we don't have the "big" album to show off for it. But I'm not competing on that sort of level anyway. It's a conscious decision. I know we're not going to cut it on the smoke bomb/dry ice kick or pull the ridiculous publicity stunts. We're divorced from that circuit.

'We have a niche and we're staying there. I don't even know if we've ever even released a single in the States ... Sure, I get played on the rock and "ethnic" shows, but I'll never get the regular pop playlists because I don't churn out music that's instant and disposable, like a hamburger. I just don't run in that race.'

Rory's interest in the cinema remained strong, as his confession that he sometimes checked into hotels using the names of actors like Alain Delon makes clear. 'While not crazy about current releases, I enjoy the films of the 1940s and 1950s, black and white crime thrillers. I also enjoy the European pictures of the 1960s: Delon, Ventura, John Paul Belmondo, those lads. I'd be lost without a video, a wonderful invention. There's nothing I like better than to be able to catch a movie at four in the morning after a show or something. I suppose I got spoiled with the twenty-four-hour, wall-to-wall TV. They show lots of movies – when you can see them through the jungle of ads. But I don't insist there's a video in my dressing room, or anything like that,' he laughs. 'I have no time for that sort of messing, although some bands have the most ridiculous riders to their contracts ... too Sodom and Gomorrah altogether.

'Take ZZ Top for instance, who I hear are playing here soon. At one stage they opened for us on a tour of the States and they were terrific. Three guys, three instruments and they just lashed it out ... smashing. They became really big and, before you knew it, they had a monstrous stage shaped like a map of Texas and a travelling Zoo with a buffalo, a buzzard, a coyote, and a longhorn steer plus a rattlesnake ... you name it, they had it. Suddenly, we were witnessing the extreme side of the Texas/Dallas oil excess. We were playing with them in Houston a while back and they met us at the airport with big slinky stretch limousines equipped with colour TVs and full bars, and though I suppose it was fun, it really got beyond the J. R. Ewing stage. There's nothing wrong with success, but when it goes to that extreme it's ridiculous. Put it this way, I'd never use a buffalo or a steer suspended over the stage, unless it could sing harmonies or hum in tune or something.'

Rory switches between electric and acoustic guitar on stage in New York (© Charlie Gili).

In June 1979 The Rory Gallagher Appreciation Society produced the first of what became a regular fanzine, *Deuce*, promising to bring news on the activities of Rory and the band and inviting contributions from fans. It was compiled from interviews with Rory and Donal Gallagher, Peter Collins, Diana Worthy and many of the other principals involved in the band. Gallagher fan Julie Gordon from Tyne and Wear was the secretary, editor and designer. The introductory issue featured profiles of Gerry McAvoy, former Sensational Alex Harvey Band drummer Ted McKenna, from Glasgow, who had made

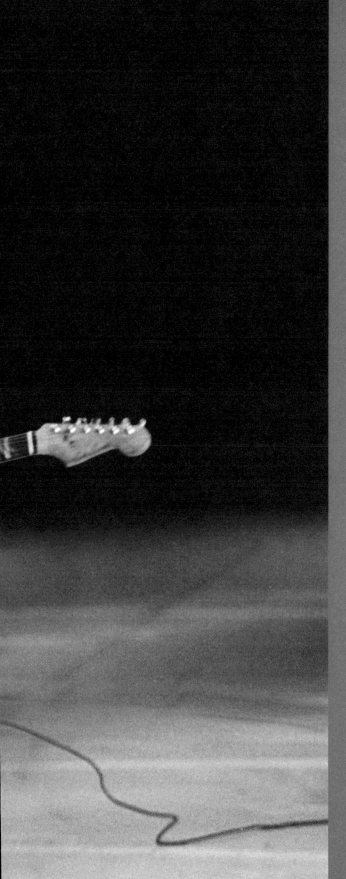

Captured on stage in Dublin
(© Colm Henry).

his debut with Rory on stage at Macroom. The Northern Ireland Guitar Society also featured in the first *Deuce*. It was formed in 1975 by Joe Cohen, John Flanigan and a number of other guitarists in Belfast. The society had over one hundred members and their Honorary President and patron was Rory Gallagher. Members of the society travelled to many of Rory's shows and hired a bus to attend the Macroom festival appearance in the summer of 1977. Julie acknowledged the worldwide nature of Rory's fan base with a special thank you to Jakob Mulder from Groningen and Kara Blok of the Dutch fan club; Marcus Gygax of the Swiss/German fan club and Mutsumi Mae in Japan.

Jakob had helped to establish the Dutch fan club in 1973 – he first saw Rory with Taste when they performed on German television in 1970 and was, like so many others across Europe, hooked. He read an advertisment in a Dutch music paper from a Belgian girl, Chantal, who wanted to write and correspond with other Gallagher fans, and after a short exchange of letters, they started up a fan club called 'Deuce', with the first issue of their fan magazine published in the summer of 1973. Many years later, Jakob published *Signals* and then, in the mid-1990s, he joined forces with Dino McGartland to bring news of Rory's music and career after his passing to his many fans through the pages of *Stagestruck*.

Rory during the session for the *Defender* album.
This photo featured in *Hot Press* (© Colm Henry).

A FTER A HIATUS OF FIVE YEARS, Rory Gallagher returned to the studio in 1987 to record *Defender*. Rory had parted company with Chrysalis Records by this time and the album was recorded for his own label, Capo Records. 'I'm not that organised,' Rory wrote in the sleeve notes, 'but I want anything that I'm doing to be under control, and I want the final say on things.' *Defender* opens with the uncompromising 'Kickback City'. One of my favourite tracks is the smoky 'Continental Op', inspired by one of his great writing heroes Dashiell Hammett. It's followed by 'Ain't No Saint', taking its inspiration from the playing of Buddy Guy and Albert Collins. I liked this track so much that when I was asked to present *Bluestime* on RTÉ Radio 1 in the early 1990s I chose it as the signature tune to honour our leading bluesman. 'Loanshark Blues' is Gallagher's homage to Chicago's Maxwell Street and inspired from the pages of one of his boyhood heroes Woody Guthrie's *Bound for Glory*, where the hero stands out from a grey backdrop and a dysfunctional society.

Rory's uncanny understanding of the political world and cloak and dagger moves that were such a part of espionage is reflected in the keenly observed 'Smear Campaign' and is a universal theme. His reading of Sonny Boy Williamson's 'Don't Start Me To Talkin' is a stand out track on *Defender*, marked by the fiery harmonica playing of the genial new Gallagher sideman, Mark Feltham, an accomplished session harmonica player who was to become a regular in Rory's band line-up. Mark is on record describing his friendship with the Cork guitarist: 'Rory was an angel – an angel. He was a fantastic person, a wonderful human being. He was one of the most wonderful men I ever met in my life. I can say that honestly and openly. He was a gentleman as in the words "gentle man", you know.'

Rory toured the album across Europe. Irish musician Barry McCabe, who played with Albatross for many years and carved his own niche across Europe as an Irish guitar troubadour, tried to catch one of the shows in West Germany.

'I had just finished some dates up in Scandinavia and stopped off in Holland on the way back home. The rest of the band headed off and I elected to stay (along with my brother) to see the first date of Rory's *Defender* tour which started in Utrecht. Rory had the choice of starting the tour a day or two earlier by doing a show in Copenhagen or doing a show in Cork, which would be recorded by RTÉ. That show became the video *Live in Cork*.

'Anyway the show in Utrecht was so good that my brother and I decided to go see a few more shows while we were there. We took in Cologne in Germany and after that headed for Berlin. By this time I had travelled and toured quite a bit of Europe but had never been to Berlin before, so it was exciting for two reasons. This was obviously before the Wall came down. So we're travelling along happy as can be and we see a sign saying that you can change money ahead. Well, we think to ourselves, we don't need to change as we're only going to West Berlin. It's a pretty long drive so we're talking and stuff and finally arrive. We decided to go straight to the concert hall, so we had the tour sheet with the name of the hall and the street address. Got there and it looked pretty deserted, no posters, nothing. Well, we had time to kill, so we decided to go check out a record store. Found one, had a look around and thought not much of a selection there. Some John Lee Hooker, Memphis Slim and Champion Jack Dupree. After that, we decided to go for a coffee. We were sitting there and I noticed when some of the other customers paid that it didn't look like DMs to me. So I said to my brother, "It looks like they're paying with different money. Maybe they have different money here even though it is the west and that's why there was the change bureau." So we're thinking, shit, what do we do now? Not really speaking any German I go to the lady behind the bar and explain that we only have DMs with us and can we pay with that. Then she said, "Don't you have any East German money?" Then it suddenly all came to light … WE WERE IN EAST GERMANY!!!!

'Oh boy, what now? We go outside and kick ourselves for not seeing it earlier. The streets were filled with Trabants (old East German car), loads of uniformed guys in the streets, 95 per cent classical music in the record store, etc. Well, you get the picture. These two paddies had somehow driven straight into East Germany. What do we do now, we thought? We're not supposed to be here. We're gonna get caught and what then? Are they gonna think we're spies or something? Are we gonna get thrown in prison? Nobody knew we were even there. So we decided the best thing for us to do was try to go back the way we came in and just explain that we had made a mistake. It's also dark by now so you can probably imagine the atmosphere in the van at that moment. We drive quite a bit and we're just about to believe that we might actually make it out (silly, I know) when a guard steps out and waves us down. He speaks no English, we speak no German, but we get the message. We shouldn't be there. Outta the van, search the van, etc. Takes about an hour and he tells us we have to go further.

'Anyway we do several stops, checks, and interrogations and to make a long story short we make it out. All we got was a 50-DM fine and a bad case of the shakes! To be honest, everyone was quite polite and even helpful. I guess the innocence that got us in got us out.

'So now "free men" we make a mad dash for the concert hall. There is the same concert hall and street name in both parts of the city. However, the one in the east is for classical concerts, hence clean and tidy and NO RORY POSTERS! We finally arrive at the hall at the very moment the doors open and thousands of happy Rory fans tumble out into the streets. We didn't get to hear A SINGLE NOTE! However, at that stage we were just happy to be there. We went in and Rory was doing a bunch of interviews so we were talking to the other guys in the band. They couldn't believe it and kept asking us were we all right and did we want something to drink and they were really helpful and considerate about the whole episode.

'So that was my Berlin experience and a (non) Rory show. I don't think I ever told Rory about it, which is probably quite a shame. Knowing his love of the spy stories, etc. he might even have got a song out of it.'

24

Fresh Evidence –
The Final Studio Album

Rory putting the Strat through
its paces on a German tour
(© Ed Erbeck).

RESH EVIDENCE was the last complete studio album recorded by Rory. Released in 1990, it is one of his finest collections, capturing the full range of his writing and playing. He appeared not only at ease with the recording process itself but with the whole challenge of locating suitable material, recording it, and finding the essence of the various tracks he had selected. Like many performing artists, however, no album was ever quite finished, even as the production plant manufactured copies and the sleeve covers were printed. The 'what if' question never left the back of Gallagher's mind. Indeed, many might claim that it dominated his entire career. This was a central driving force of Rory – to get that piece of music nailed down. In his final years, this resulted in a variety of fears that became almost obsessive compulsive and meant that, when he was taken ill, his reserves of strength, both physical and mental, were under some considerable pressure to cope.

Rory took the album to North America, talking to John Sakamoto of the *Toronto Sun* about his increasing fear of flying. 'We've been doing lots of dates in Europe flying in small planes. We had a couple of bad flights, at least from my point of view … It's like any phobia, it goes away eventually, although even flying here [to Toronto from Minneapolis] yesterday, I had to kind of brace myself, you know.

'We were offered American dates last year, but the flying thing held me back then, plus we were dissatisfied with one or two of the tours we'd done in America where most of the dates were supporting some stadium rock act. We were getting less than decent conditions – no lights, no monitors, six feet of stage.' On this tour, however, Rory and the band were headlining clubs and small venues. 'Certainly the success of people like Stevie Ray Vaughan and George Thorogood and Jeff Healey helped, but I think also that a lot of young people were dissatisfied with the "video" kind of music that was coming out. I think that they were looking for the raw bones and roots of rock again.' Commenting on 'Kid Gloves', about a boxer who refuses to take a dive, Sakamoto wondered if it reflected Rory's not yielding to the fashions and demands of the music biz. 'It's written the way Jerry Lee Lewis would view the music business. It's a kind of statement of defiance against the way things are, and you can't put a good man down and all that. It's also done tongue-in-cheek, if I was as bitter as I am in the song,' he said laughing softly, 'I'd really be in trouble.'

Jas Obrecht, the long-time editor of *Guitar Player* magazine, was to interview Rory in America in 1991. He asked him first why his music always seemed to gravitate towards roots American music.

Rory: 'Even though you develop as a player over the years and become influenced by different things, you have to keep to the heart of what you started with, that initial vision of music. I grew up in Ireland where folk and traditional music is very close at hand, but I really wasn't turned on until I heard American music via Lonnie Donegan, who was doing Woody Guthrie songs, Leadbelly. Of course, I also heard the early rockers ... Elvis Presley, Eddie Cochran, Chuck Berry, so it was a mixture of folk, blues, and rock from America. I just followed it through and eventually learned who's who in the spectrum of things, the prime movers and the copyists. In early blues, for instance, everyone's stating that Robert Johnson is the virtuoso of that era, but Son House was very important at the time.

'All young rock and blues players should dig deeper, back beyond the obvious blues stars like B. B. King and Buddy Guy, who are great. I'm very interested in the country blues and electrified country blues, such as Big Joe Williams. I also like all the slide players from Earl Hooker through Muddy Waters. Robert Nighthawk is a favourite of mine, and I eventually discovered Tampa Red. That guitar lick that Muddy Waters is known for came from Tampa Red.

'So this folk music tradition of passing on, picking up, and stealing goes on like mad! If I'm doing a blues number, I can do it very traditional if I want to; I can also add my own twists to it.'

Jas Obrecht felt that this latter quality was reflected on many tracks on *Fresh Evidence*.

Rory: 'Yeah, "Empire State Express", for instance, was done in one take on purpose. I do it close enough to Son House's style, but to sing it in the tempo I had to slightly adjust the rhythm. It's a great but very overlooked song in Open G tuning [D G D G B D low to high]. "Ghost Blues" is quite traditional in its approach with the National; it's also tuned to Open G. The guitar in "Middle Name" is more like a Slim Harpo record, so there are all kinds of references.

'Besides a few rock tracks, the rest are very much in the blues field. The album before this, *Defender*, had a lot of blues elements as well, but it was more of a rock production, whereas with this new one we didn't overdo the compression or the cleaning up. We left it fairly woolly and casual, which suits the songs. Still, I hope people catch up

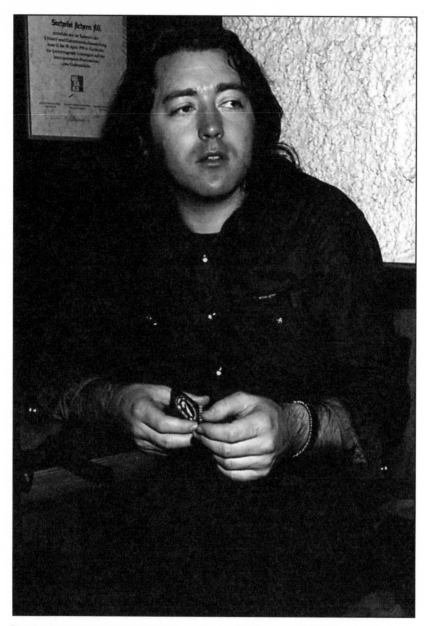

Rory backstage in pensive mood while on the road in Germany (© Ed Erbeck).

on *Defender*, because it is still quite current in our set, even though we move the repertoire around every night. Nine times out of ten, I work off the top of my head and we move from album to album.'

Obrecht next asked what a Rory Gallagher guitar solo should be about.

Rory: 'I try to split the difference between being fairly clever and technical and still primitive. I used to always go for "live" leads ... mistakes and all ... just for the feel. Now if a certain song needs a very melodic solo, I'm prepared to work on it over and over. But I try not to get in the habit in studio of dropping in [overdubbing] because it's very tempting to get the perfect solo. As a rule, I try to keep a grip on technology so it doesn't take the human factor out of it.'

On his slide style and approach, Rory had this to say:

Rory: 'Pick and fingers. I also vary the slides. Sometimes I use a Coricidin bottle on my ring finger, sometimes my small finger. I use a brass slide if I'm playing a National. If I'm playing a straight [standard tuned] electric, I use a steel bottleneck. The sound of glass is more smooth and sweet. The brass or copper is very harsh! Good if you want to get the Son House sort of attack, but it's almost too harsh to use all the time. Steel is a good compromise, and socket wrenches are ideal. I have a 5/8th or 7/8th, because John Hammond told me he was using one, and Lowell George had one as well. They're fantastic, but you really need very heavy strings. And if you're playing more than a couple of numbers, they do wear your small finger down, and you don't want to be tiring your hand. I use a Gretsch Corvette for slide in Open G or A [E A E A B E]; and that's got strings from .013 to .050. The action on my regular guitars is quite high and the strings are .010 to .044 so it's ok for slide. I can cope with both.'

In 1999 I was in touch with Jas Obrecht about the possibility of his coming to Cork to speak about the influence of Tampa Red and others on Rory (Jas is the world's authority on Tampa Red). He was very interested in joining what he called the 'Gallagher gathering' but, sadly, it never came to pass. He did, however, remember Rory fondly, as 'a warm, sweet human being and just a terrific guitarist. His "Tatto'd Lady" guitar solo was a lightning bolt from Heaven.'

Another year on from the release of *Fresh Evidence* and Donal Gallagher got a call from Bob Dylan's office. 'This was in or around '92,' Donal remembered, 'and he wanted to get a copy of *Live in Europe* on CD. Dylan's office had contacted our record company in America who said that they didn't know the title. This is what you are up against with record companies. I dropped a line and said "here you go, here's *Live in Europe* as you wanted, but here also is Rory's latest album, *Fresh Evidence*". So, we had a lovely note back. I had

Above and facing page: Rory entertains and captivates his German fans (© Ed Erbeck).

enquired as to why he wanted *Live in Europe*. Dylan was going to do a version of "I Could Have Had Religion", which is quite an honour by another writer like Dylan. "Rory," he said, 'I Could Have Had Religion' – you wrote that song?" Rory said, "Well, yeah I did." "But you've put it down as traditional, as an old blues song, as a traditional piece of music." And Rory said, "I got a verse out of a blues book of poetry and developed the song from there." "You actually had me fooled," Dylan said, "I thought this was one of the ghost blues songs of America and I wanted to do a version of it. In doing my research on it, I found you had written it and Rory, the reason I didn't put it on the record, I'd love to have done it, but if I had put it down I would have put it in as a Bob Dylan traditional blues song and that wouldn't have been fair to you." His parting words were "Why don't we get together when you are out in the States next and we'll record something?" Sadly, that was never to be.'

25

Ghost Blues

Rory in the City Hall, Cork, in 1992 (© Tony O'Connell).

N NOVEMBER 1993 Rory Gallagher was invited to headline the first Cork Regional Technical College Arts Festival. It was an intimate, acoustic gig. I remember travelling down from Dublin and meeting filmmaker and musician Philip King as we alighted at Kent Station in Cork. We decided that a stroll to the Moynihan's Long Valley Bar on Winthrop Street was on the cards, and, as we walked the streets of Cork, we reminisced on when we'd last seen Rory and how he was. We had both caught his appearance at the Guinness Temple Bar Blues Festival in the summer of 1992 in College Green in Dublin. Little did we realise we were on our way to see Rory's last concert in his homeland.

Rory's uncle Jimmy Roche had been, for many years, the principal of the Cork Regional Technical College – now the Cork Institute of Technology – and Donal explained how the Arts Festival appearance came about.

'Uncle Jimmy was always keen to expand the Arts element of the college. He was also keen to bring in new learning like the technology we were applying to the gigs on the audio and logistics side of it. These were areas he was keen to open up courses on. Jimmy had been a huge musical influence on Rory as well, because to get his education he had gone to Canada and the United States as a student and worked in the automobile/car plants.

'He actually brought back the catalogue of Jimmie Rodgers/Hank Snow and various others. He was a very fine singer and, as youngsters, we would listen to him at family parties. This was the thing, we were trying to hear the Lonnie Donegan, cowboy Roy Rogers/Gene Autry songs – this was first hand; somebody had brought it off the boat back from America, and dollars and cents, and the feel of American music became more real because of and thanks to Jimmy Roche.

'The first leather jacket Rory ever saw was from my Uncle Jimmy, there was a huge *grá* for Jimmy in that regard. Sadly, when Jimmy passed on rather suddenly, Rory took it very much to heart. They were very, very close. Something had to be done, some sort of memorial. I think there was a "Ghost Blues" element to it, that Rory felt, I'll do this, it's passing it on.

'It was a tense night but a great night in the end and it was also what I had been urging Rory to do, which was to dispense with carrying a band for a while because of all that entails. It's a very expensive thing to stay touring, to stay on the road, and particularly the way Rory was very generous to his musicians, contrary to what some publications might like to say.

'Rory funded everything about their lifestyles, and it actually had caused huge stresses, because you have the taxes, the accountants – all the things Rory did not want to deal with, had to be addressed. I had said if you dispense with the band and just go on the road and do an acoustic set, bring say a "Lou Martin" on piano. In fact, we had this conversation after the gig that night, where he could go on a tour that didn't require a large PA, trucking, catering, transport, and all that stuff, get back very much to the folky roots of things. After that night in November 1993, he was very keen to go that route, but time ran on, Rory wanted to get back in the studio, the electrics came back out and it wasn't to be.'

Following the concert in Bishopstown, Cork, that night, which also featured Mark Feltham on harmonica and the aforementioned Lou Martin on piano, we headed for Jury's Hotel on the Western Road where the band were staying. I had travelled to Cork to cover Rory's appearance for a radio programme I was producing, titled *Both Sides Now*, presented on alternate nights by Paschal Mooney and Aonghus MacAnally (an odd concoction) on RTÉ Radio 1. Sitting up into the small hours with Rory and Lou Martin we chatted about Muddy Waters, Howlin' Wolf, Lafayette Leake, Pinetops Smith and Perkins, the Chess Brothers and Chicago blues, Bruce Bastin and his *Red River Blues* covering the Carolinas. Lou headed for his *leaba* at around three in the morning, Rory and I chatted on for another hour or two. I still had, at the back of my mind, the niggling matter of that 'interview' for the programme – the reason for the journey to Rory's hometown. We agreed that I'd drop by Rory's room and we'd record a short piece around lunchtime. What follows is that interview – the final interview that Rory recorded on Irish soil prior to his untimely demise.

Well Rory, you're here in Cork, back in your hometown again and it was a wonderful homecoming. You're here for the Regional Technical College Arts Fest, tell me a little about how that all came about. There's a family connection there?

'Well, Matt Cranitch [of Na Filí] approached my brother about doing an acoustic show as part of the Arts Week here at the college and I was delighted to, you know, take it on as I have family connections there. My uncle Jimmy was the principal there and I have done a few acoustic shows over the years, like in Montreux and one or two TV shows in Holland [Rory neglects to mention, I'm sure out of modesty, his barnstorming acoustic session for Richard Digance on Capitol Radio in the 1980s]. It's been quite a few years, and it was great to look through the catalogue of songs that I know and a few that I haven't played live and luckily there was quite a, you know, most of it was bluesy, I had one or two more folk things there, and it was a bit of a challenge.

'One's hometown show is a joy, yet it's very tense, you don't want to let anybody down, your family, or the audience, or yourself. So we brought Mark Feltham, the great harmonica player, along to help out on some songs and Lou Martin, my old buddy from the old days to play some piano and to open up the show. I was a little apprehensive but once we got there and checked it out, the audience was beautiful and warm. It was serious but there was an element of kind of fun as well, which doesn't hurt. It wasn't exactly a Segovia recital, but it's great for me 'cause I can write and play but until I get on stage, the X factor [before the term became demeaned] comes into being, because an audience, you can really draw from them and get inspiration and fire and all kinds of qualities that you think you have lost or can't find. I think that's the problem with studio work, it's that you have to dig all that out of your innards, whereas if you have an audience there and they are demanding and also you get the odd comment or the odd yelp and if it's good-natured it spurs you on. We had a great night, and I'm relieved and happy and still getting rid of the perspiration but I'm fine otherwise.'

There is no doubt that there was a great response from the audience, also the fact that you moved from one acoustic instrument to another, and the lovely thing as well that you picked up the mandolin. I haven't seen you play that in a long, long time.

'I don't know, I play it sort of in a straight, I'm not like a great single string player, I play it more like Yank Rachell, who was one of the great blues mandolin players, but then I play sort of triplets and I just have my own way of doing it. I'm hoping to include it on the new acoustic album. Bozouki as well, I've picked it up lately, having promised myself for years, but I tune it my own sort of way, and I started the show tonight with "I'm Not Awake Yet" which I haven't played for a hundred years.

'It was nice because it gave it a wee bit of an historical kind of pitch and I did songs I haven't done for ages like "Bankers Blues" by Big Bill Broonzy and I also did a bit of "She Moved Through the Fair" which sort of segued into "Out on the Western Plain" and we did one or two that we haven't often done like "I'm Ready", a Muddy Waters song [on which Rory had played guitar during Muddy's *London Sessions*].

'I swapped around. I had two acoustics, different tunings for different songs, and I had the old brown National, the early 1930s model, only problem with that is that it's quite hard to amplify it by putting pick-ups on it. Just no one seems to have beaten that tone yet, but it's down to your "black belt" fingers and you have to hit them hard. There is great character to that instrument, you can't "Minnie Mouse" with it! You really have to go for it, but I love that guitar, it's, I mean it's probably worth "god knows what". But when I bought it [with John Hammond, scion of a great blues family, in New York's Lower East Side] I didn't know what a bargain I was getting and it's great I love it, you know?'

You are about to go into the studio and you mentioned earlier that you have some preparatory work done. I believe you have two albums worth of material in the works at the minute. Obviously you've been busy writing over the past few months.

'I did a lot of writing earlier in the year, in fact, I was back here in Cork for a while and it's quite hard to write in London sometimes because it's quite a stressful city and so on. But I was going to do this acoustic album many years ago, but the trouble is that I didn't just want to do ten country blues covers, which would be grand you know, but I actually hit a point where I wrote, we'll say, nine or ten acoustic songs that are blues and are folk and beyond, but that would stand up in court. That doesn't mean that I won't do one or two traditional songs as well. So I'm looking forward to that, and I'm hoping to play twelve-string as well, mix and match with acoustic piano and double bass and whatever. And on the electric album as well I'm just sussing out between, a lot of songs are country blues in an electric way á la early John Lee Hooker (Real Folk Blues) period, just a few Rhythm and Blues sort of songs. I've had to really watch it because over the years I've written acoustic songs and then I've transported them to the electric and the next thing you have lost a great acoustic to get a good electric, but this time they seem to be keeping themselves to one side of the tennis court, and so it's working out well.

'The next step is to get a good engineer who will understand what we are trying to do rather than state of the art forty-eight track, endless mixing and God knows what, so we've been working on it and taping things and adjusting it, so I'm looking forward to that, it's, because well *Fresh Evidence* isn't that long ago, but it's long enough, really isn't it? I don't know it must be …?

It's about three years now since Fresh Evidence.

'God that's frightening, but its good because new material just changes the whole picture, because it puts … it's invigorating, plus it's almost like having a baby type of thing! You have to, it's a great relief if you are somewhat happy with it and the people like it as well. I think my favourite track from *Fresh Evidence*, if I had to pick one, is "Ghost Blues". It's a bit long really but I'm still very fond of that sort of "Redemption Blues", Reverend Robert Wilkins influenced song.

Well, I can tell you this much, that I know a lot of your fans certainly all over Ireland and overseas will be looking forward to hearing those new albums, which hopefully will be released sometime next year in 1994, but for the time being, Rory, a great pleasure to see you again and congratulations and thank you for a wonderful night.

'Thank you very much Marcus, it was my pleasure.'

26

I'll Admit You're Gone

Tom O'Driscoll carries Rory's beloved Stratocaster at the musician's funeral on 19 June 1995 in Cork.

RORY GALLAGHER was in Dublin for the first Guinness Temple Bar Blues Festival in August 1992. It would be his last show in the capital. In a revealing interview with Joe Jackson of *The Irish Times*, he spoke about what he described as his 'black cat feelings'. The life of a touring musician is often a solitary and remote one, filling the time between performances when you know little else in your working regime for over three decades. Rory told Jackson that he tuned into those black cat feelings in a way that was beyond his control. 'You have to step over a certain line, not necessarily to connect with evil, but to take yourself as close to the brink as you can to give the music that essential edge. It's a dangerous balance you have to try to maintain.'

The 'Black Cat Moan', a howl of despair, has long been a part of the blues canon, as evidenced by this song recorded by the former Yardbird Jeff Beck with former Vanilla Fudge members Tim Bogert and Carmine Appice as Beck, Bogert and Appice.

'Black Cat Moan'

Looky here

Sunshine coming over the hills
Through my window pane
Sunshine coming over the hills
Might as well be pain
Got the black cat moan
Got the black cat moan
Got the black cat moan
Got the black cat moan

Laying by the side of the road
With the devils flying by
Looks like my head is gonna roll
Don't know the reasons why
Got the black cat moan
Got the black cat moan
Got the black cat moan cause I wanna go home
Got the black cat moan

Going back to Memphis
To find my sugar ray
Going back to Memphis
Cause that's where I want to be
Got the black cat moan
Got the black cat moan
Got the black cat moan I wanna go home
Got the black cat moan

(Traditional/Copyright Control)

Gallagher told Joe Jackson that he was not the kind of musician who believed in taking on 'the excesses of Jimi Hendrix in the hope of giving his music that edge. I'm not saying Hendrix sold his soul to the devil but he did think – "I'm a meteor and I'm going to burn out young, yet even if I die I'm going to play as no one ever played before." He paid for that aim with his life. He was as demonic as Johnson in his own way but I never really was tempted to try those excesses. And the key reason was absolute fear, fear of that darkness taking over.'

That fear was further fuelled by 'seeing people like Hendrix and Paul Kossoff of Free die as they did. I'm not saying Phil Lynott went that way, but I saw him weeks before he died and I got a cold feeling of his imminent death. And despite that rock and roll line, "die young and leave a good looking corpse", to me there's nothing glamorous about dying young, even if the journey makes you the greatest musician in the world.

'I've never come close to dying, no, but I have come close to fearing it. Maybe that's part of the Celtic inheritance, feeling you are immersed in bad luck and death will be the only way out, whatever the cause. But, sure, I take a drink, yet not to excess. The idea that you can't play the blues unless you're an alcoholic may be part of rock and roll mythology, but it's not true. I certainly don't need to be drunk to play. The idea is nonsense and, potentially, a lethal notion to be selling to young musicians.'

Talking to Jackson about the latest album *Edged in Blue*, a compilation of his favourite blues recordings from his back catalogue, Rory described how 'The blues can be sexist but that simply reflects a lack of political knowledge at the time most of the songs were written.

But when I write a song like "Continental Op", although it is a blues song I make sure it is in no way connected to what are worrying questions about sexism in blues lyrics and also violence towards women you find in songs by Big Bill Broonzy and company. As a white European, I have tried to take the songs into areas beyond the "I am a Little Red Rooster" department. And I feel proud of having at least attempted that, even if the songs aren't hits. I do feel I have advanced the blues in that way, politically.

'There's no doubt when I first got a guitar as a school kid in Cork it rounded out my life completely, became an instant friend. And although I have had relationships, I probably did put my career first in terms of touring and my attention to the music. Others may be in a hurry to marry me off, but I really don't like discussing my private life. Not just in terms of the media, but even with my friends. I am a private person. I don't even discuss my relationships or my feelings with them.'

Donal confirmed this in an interview with Michael Ross in *The Sunday Times* three years after the musician's death. 'Whatever he was feeling, good or bad, he kept very much to himself. I can't say that we ever had an in-depth personal conversation. There wasn't a lot said between us. There was a kind of telepathy between us, though. I'd say he was extremely lonely but it was hard to tell because he was so private. He was tremendously melancholic and he was never satisfied with anything he did.'

In mid-1994, Rory's health began to deteriorate and he became puffy and slightly bloated, which was completely out of character. 'I felt he was giving up,' said Donal. 'His physical exhaustion had led to mental exhaustion. I think, with hindsight, that the poor man had had a series of nervous breakdowns that were not visible to other people. When I saw how serious the situation had become, I reckoned it was better for him to go out and work. He had been under strain during his time off the road in London, trying to create new music. It had become counter-productive. Rory's natural cure was to tour, get his adrenalin going and use his energy productively. But that was the dilemma. The thing that made him better also made him worse through exhaustion.'

In January 1995, Rory's ill health caused him to abandon a tour of the Netherlands halfway through. Donal again: 'When he started having abdominal pains, which, with hindsight, was probably the first sign of his liver trouble, he was prescribed paracetamol, which, where a liver is damaged, can cause more damage. I wish more checks had been made at the time.'

In Easter 1995, I was returning to Cork from compering the annual Burnley Blues Festival (I had moved to Rory's home town by the Lee Delta the previous year to work with RTÉ Cork). In the departures lounge of Dublin airport I met up with Donal and Rory's mother Monica (Mona). Monica was returning to Cork and Donal was going back to his home in London. Donal took me to one side and explained that Rory had just undergone major surgery. He'd had a liver transplant, but was doing well post-operatively and his doctors were encouraged by his progress. Donal felt that his brother was in good spirits and pleased that he was receiving excellent care and attention in King's College Hospital.

It was, in fact, only after his admission to King's College Hospital in March that the full extent of Rory's ill health became clear. Donal: 'It was only then that he got the medical care he needed, the surgeon who performed the operation was staggered that such a young man needed a new liver. This liver damage was compounded by drink, though Rory was not the heavy drinker he was rumoured to be.'

But Rory did not recover and after nearly three months in intensive care, Rory is thought to have contracted a drug resistant infection. On 14 June 1995 Rory Gallagher died due to complications following his liver transplant.

'I didn't believe he would die, or I didn't want to. He deteriorated rapidly in the end because his immune system was exhausted. They pumped him full of antibiotics but it was no use. With hindsight, I would have done some things differently, but I don't blame myself. You can't change someone if they don't want to change. Rory wasn't going to change for anybody,' said Donal.

Three days later, on Saturday 17 June, thousands of Corkonians both young and old thronged the streets of the city to pay their respects to their hero, a guitarist, musician, composer, and performer who strode the stages of the world with his unique performances as a cultural ambassador for Cork.

His funeral mass took place two days later in the Church of the Descent of the Holy Ghost in Dennehy's Cross, within walking distance of the city centre in the suburbs of Wilton. Prior to the funeral mass, the Bishop of Cork and Ross, Dr John Buckley, had this to say: 'Over the years I've known how popular Rory was and his music, how much he was appreciated by the people of Cork, indeed, by generations of young Cork people, an internationally known figure, of course, a man of talent, a man of great skill especially in his chosen career of music. Rory was a very good man, very good to his family, his dear mother Monica and very good to many charitable causes, so on an occasion like this, we are sad at the passing of a young man at such a young age and I suppose it's very appropriate today that we should all come together.

'A huge crowd of young people have gathered and Cork people who have listened to his music, and I think it shows the esteem that Rory is held in his native city of Cork. We are proud of him, proud of his talents, he was a Corkman and Rory was also proud of his own native city and availed of every opportunity to come back and give those enjoyable end of year concerts. His death is lamented, not alone here in Cork, but indeed throughout the world, large numbers of people/musicians have travelled to be present on this sad occasion.'

Ronnie Drew of The Dubliners, a friend of Rory's throughout the years, was one of the pall bearers. He also gave a reading at the funeral mass from the *Book of Wisdom*: 'He accepted them as a holocaust, the souls of the virtuous are in the hands of God, no torment shall ever touch them. The eyes of the unwise they did appear to die, their going looked like a disaster, the leaving us, like an annihilation, for they are in peace.'

27
Legacy

Rory's Stratocaster (© Fin Costello).

ORY WAS GONE, but his music and memory remain, in the many posthumously released albums, memorial lectures, fan magazines like *Stagestruck*, run by Dino and Annie McGartland, websites such as roryon.com celebrating his music, and places and plaques carrying his name, like the Rory Gallagher Music Library in Cork City Library. Then, there is the influence he had on the next generation of guitarists, including The Edge, Slash, Johnny Fean, Johnny Marr, Declan Sinnott, Dave McHugh and fiddler Martin Hayes, and the example he set for bands like U2 as Ireland's first international rock star. Most importantly, however, Rory's music lives on in the hearts of his fans and in the tribute concerts and festivals that are a constant across Ireland, the UK and Europe.

As Gary Moore, guitarist with Skid Row and Thin Lizzy, remarked following Rory Gallagher's untimely death in London on 14 June 1995. 'The sad and ironic thing about his death is that, with all these Blues revivals going on, Rory's time had come around again.'

One of the people to take a lead in honouring Rory was Tony Moore, who opened The Rory Gallagher Bar in the east Cork town of Midleton in 1996. In a talk he gave on the ninth anniversary of the guitarist's death, Tony described coming across Rory for the first time. Not particularly impressed by the showbands of the 1960s, Tony and his best pal decided to look elsewhere for musical sustenance. 'We found it up in Cork city in places like the Shandon Boat Club, small venues featuring bands like the Axills and Sleepy Hollow. These bands were raw, bluesy, urban, and a million miles away from the sounds in Redbarn in Youghal. My mate was Donal Murray, my first cousin: we grew up together. One evening we were drifting aimlessly around town when we passed a hall, we heard music and in we went – it was a private party and on the stage was a long-haired guitarist whom Donal recognised as Rory Gallagher. We stayed for the gig. I guess it was 1965 – The Beatles, the Stones, Dylan, and the Animals – brilliant bands and songwriters were dominating music. For me, 1965 to 1975 was a golden era when classic albums and singles were released almost every month.'

In 1985, Tony opened the Meeting Place bar on Connolly Street in Midleton, regularly featuring live music and hosting the Midleton Folk Club. 'When alterations were carried out to the bar in 1996,' Tony explained, 'my brother-in-law Seamus McLellan, head bar man, suggested we call the new area The Rory Gallagher Bar. A local band, Tres Hombres, who were inspired by Rory's playing opened it on his anniversary on 14 June 1996. Members of the Gallagher family attended the opening, including Rory's mother and Donal who delivered a welcome address.'

Tony has been playing host to tribute bands and performers inspired by the great Cork musician ever since. 'Bands like the Juke Joints from Holland and Tony Dowler from the UK would come over and do four gigs. I would depend on friends in other towns and venues to get three gigs to cover the costs and then have the band finish on a Sunday night in Midleton. I often took gambles on foreign tribute bands looking for tours, like the Mississippi Sheiks from Sweden, Laundromat from Holland, and Bad Penny from Germany. Luckily, the vast majority of the tributes were classic gigs.'

Perhaps some of the best bands to perform Rory Gallagher's repertoire were Cabra's finest Dave McHugh and Jed Thomas, from Wales, as well as Brute Force and Ignorance from Germany, a sure sign of his immense popularity in that country.

Tony has also encouraged Irish fans of Rory's to travel to and support tribute festivals across Europe, at places like Dukinfield near Manchester, Leeuwarden in Holland (organised by Klaas and Annette Spijker), and Wiesbaden in Germany. Karlheinz Bilstein, from Wiesbaden, is one of the Corkman's most dedicated fans. Christened '20 Dollar Bill' by Rory, Karlheinz has one of the most extensive collections of Gallagher memorabilia, which he shares with Rory fans at the tribute shows organised in his home town in the heart of Germany.

These tribute concerts are a deeply emotional experience for many of those attending, and lifelong friendships have been inspired by a shared love by Rory's music. Gordon and Dorothy Morris from the north of England, now living in Cumbria, are two Rory fans who have become dear friends of mine. They got to know Rory well in the late 1970s and stayed close friends. They were in regular correspondence with Rory's mother following his death.

Gordon and Dorothy met Rory for the first time after a gig at the Birmingham NEC in 1978. They happened to be staying in the same hotel as the band and, after bumping into Rory in the foyer, went on to enjoy an amazing night with their hero.

Gordon remembers: 'I was very nervous at first but there was no need because as soon as I got to Rory it was like meeting any guy from the back streets of Manchester, just so down-to-earth, so humble, so friendly. I couldn't believe it. Just seeing him – the wild man on stage, this rock God, you sort of expect a bit of arrogance I suppose but there was not a sign of arrogance. We just shook hands and I told him I'd enjoyed the gig and he was quite interested from the start to know if all the people, particularly at the back of the hall, had heard it ok, were the acoustics good. He was very concerned about that.

'He was also furious that they had put on the house lights when his set finished when ordinarily he'd play two or three encores. "I'm never going to play here again," he said.

'We were invited up to his room and Rory was chatting as though he'd known us all our lives. Then back to the bar and I remember distinctly at some stage he was chatting about redecorating the toilet in his flat, and telling us why he preferred living in a flat, to actually buying a house. The whole thing was so surreal ... how could this God be talking to me ... a mere amoeba, about things like that! Eventually, I thought "Well, we've taken up enough of his time, we'll go to the room". So I just had a quiet word with Dorothy and we made our excuses and got up to leave. And he said "Will you be coming to see me on any other leg of the tour?" So I said, "Yeah indeed, we'll come to see you in Brighton." He said, "Have you got tickets?" And I said, "Not yet, but I'll be going for them tomorrow morning". He said, "No you won't. From now on, your name is on the door. Wherever you go, your name is on the door. If you have any problem, just go to the stage door, ask for me personally and I'll sort it." Which I just could not believe, that's just the measure of the man, the first meeting – so friendly, so open.'

Gordon also remembers the first time they actually saw Rory. 'It was in Manchester in 1970 at the Free Trade Hall and it was the Taste/Stone the Crows/Jake Holmes tour. The hall was filled, mostly with university students, and you could dig your way through the heavy aroma of various illegal substances. The guy standing next to me was telling me that Rory was a very popular figure in the university but nothing could have prepared me for what was about to happen when Rory took to the stage. After a brief announcement, this young man ran onto the stage, long hair flowing behind him, checked shirt, blue jeans, Stratocaster in hand.

'He plugged in and the hall exploded with the most energetic enthusiasm I had ever seen from a performer. His music filled my every sense and it awoke in me emotions that, I am sure, would otherwise have remained dormant forever. I was mesmerised by Rory's playing and by the raw passion in his vocals. I was completely blown away, not really believing what I was experiencing as my mind struggled to make sense of the power of Rory's music. The performance was to be massively influential in my life, and the same can be said for Dorothy who was equally hypnotised by Rory and his particular brand of music. We left the Free Trade Hall sweating and exhausted, totally high on nothing but the music. That night literally changed our lives as we began to seek out every Rory gig that we could possibly get to, which eventually numbered in excess of two hundred, including the four blissful "Guitarists Evenings" with Rory, Juan Martin, David Lindley, and Richard Thompson. During all that time, we never saw the same show twice; each individual night was unique, in the way that Rory would play any given song in a slightly different way, even changing the lyrics around. We never saw Rory sit back resting on his laurels. He refused to take the easy option of playing by numbers, as he genuinely sought to give 100 per cent satisfaction to his various audiences at each and every show. I have seen many other gigs by various musicians but I have yet to see another performer come even close.

'A year or so after Rory's death,' I remember asking Dorothy what she missed most about Rory, and she immediately replied "his smile" … I choked back a tear because I too missed his smile above all else, anyone who saw his lovely welcoming smile off stage will understand. To sum up Rory, if you were to write down every attribute you could think of to make up the perfect person or friend, you would probably look at the list and be convinced that no one could quite match up … but in fact, you have would have listed something approaching the gentle man that was Rory Gallagher.'

Rory tackles that bottleneck.

RORY GALLAGHER & TASTE DISCOGRAPHY

(courtesy Dino McGartland)

LABEL	CAT NO.	TITLE

TASTE SINGLES

Major Minor	MM 560	Blister On The Moon / Born On The Wrong Side Of Town (4/ 68)
Polydor	56313	Born On The Wrong Side Of Time / Same Old Story (3/ 69)
Major Minor	MM 718	Blister On The Moon / Born On The Wrong Side Of Town (/ 68)
Polydor	POSP 609	Blister On The Moon / Sugar Mama / Catfish / On The Boards (7'/ 82)
Polydor	POSPX 609	Blister On The Moon / Sugar Mama / Catfish / On The Boards (12'/ 82)

TASTE LPS

Polydor	583 042	*Taste* (4/69)
Polydor	583 083	*On The Boards* (1/70, No.18)
Polydor	2310 082	*Live Taste* (2/71)
Polydor	2383 120	*Taste Live At The Isle of Wight* (8/72, No.41)
Polydor	2384 076	*Taste* (1977)

TASTE CDS

Polydor	841 600-2	*Taste* (8/92)
Polydor	841 599-2	*On The Boards* (4/94)
Polydor	841 602-2	*Live Taste* (/94)
Polydor	841 601-2	*Taste Live At The Isle of Wight* (4/94)
Polydor	521 999-2	*The Best Of Taste* (/2000)

RORY GALLAGHER SINGLES

Polydor	2814 004	It's You / Just The Smile / Sinnerboy (1/71)
Chrysalis	CDV 102	Souped Up Ford / I Take What I Want (11/75)
Chrysalis	CHS 2281 (1978)	Shadow Play / Souped Up Ford / Brute Force & Ignorance
Chrysalis	CHS 2364	Philby / Hellcat / Country Mile (8/79)
Chrysalis	CHS 2453	Wayward Child (live) / Keychain (8/80)
Chrysalis	CHS 2466	Hellcat / Nothin' But The Devil (/ 80)
Chrysalis	CHS 2612	Big Guns / The Devil Made Me Do It (6/82)
Chrysalis	CXP 2281	Shadow Play / Brute Force & Ignorance / Moonchild / Souped Up Ford (10/78)
Capo	82876 507752	Wheel Within Wheels / Going To My Hometown (2003)

RORY GALLAGHER LPS

Polydor	2383 044	*Rory Gallagher* (5/71, No.32)
Polydor	2383 076	*Deuce* (11/71, No.39)
Polydor	2383 112	*Live In Europe* (gatefold sleeve, 5/72, No.9)
Polydor	2383 189	*Blueprint* (2/73, No.12)
Polydor	2383 230	*Tattoo* (8/73, No.32)
Polydor	2659 031	*Irish Tour '74* (2-LP, 7/74, No.36)
Polydor	2383 315	*Sinner & Saint* (compilation, 1975)
Chrysalis	CHR 1098	*Against The Grain* (with inner sleeve, 10/75)
Polydor	2383 376	*The Story So Far* (compilation, 2/76)
Chrysalis	CHE 1124	*Calling Card* (with inner sleeve, 10/76, No.32)
Chrysalis	CHR 1170	*Photo-Finish* (with inner sleeve, 10/76)
Polydor	2384 079	*Live* (compilation, 1977)
Chrysalis	CHR 1235	*Top Priority* (with inner sleeve, 9/79, No.56)
Chrysalis	CHR 1280	*Stage Struck* (with inner sleeve, 9/80, No.40)
Chrysalis	CHR1359	*Jinx* (with inner sleeve, 4/82, No.68)
Capo / Demon XFIEND 98		*Defender* (free 7': Seems To Me / No Peace For The Wicked) (7/87)
Capo	CAPO LP 14	*Fresh Evidence* (5/90)
Demon / FIEND 719		*Edged In Blue* (compilation, 6/92)

RORY GALLAGHER LP REISSUES

Chrysalis	CHR 1253	*Blueprint* (1979)
Chrysalis	CHR 1254	*Deuce* (1979)
Chrysalis	CHR 1256	*Irish Tour '74* (2-LP, 1979)
Chrysalis	CHR 1257	*Live In Europe* (1979)
Chrysalis	CHR 1258	*Rory Gallagher* (1979)
Chrysalis	CHR 1259	*Tattoo* (1979)
Demon	FIEND 123	*Top Priority* (5/88)
Demon	FIEND 120	*Irish Tour '74* (2-LP, 5/88)
Demon	FIEND 126	*Jinx* (5/88)
Castle	TFOLP 20	*Live In Europe / Stage Struck* (2-LP, 5/88)
Castle	TFOPL 21	*Tattoo / Blueprint* (2-LP, 7/89)
Essential	ESSLP 143	*Calling Card* (4/91)
Castle	CLALP 233	*Against The Grain* (5/91)

RORY GALLAGHER CDS

Capo / Demon FIENDCD98		*Defender* (7/87)
Demon FIENDCD 123		*Top Priority* (5/88)
Demon FIENDCD 120		*Irish Tour '74* (2-CD, 5/88)
Demon FIENDCD 126		*Jinx* (5/88)

Castle	TFO CD 20	*Live In Europe / Stage Struck* (2-CD, 5/89)
Castle	TFO CD 21	*Tattoo / Blueprint* (2-CD, 7/89)
Capo	CAPO CD 14	*Fresh Evidence* (5/90)
Castle	CLACD 233	*Against The Grain* (5/91)
Demon	RORY G 1	*Rory Gallagher* (4-CD box-set includes *Defender*, *Irish Tour '74*, *Top Priority* and *Jinx*, 1991)
Essential	ESSCD 143	*Calling Card* (4/91)
Demon	FIENDCD 719	*Edged In Blue* (6/ 92)
Essential	ESSCD 155	*Fresh Evidence* (10/92)
Essential	ESBCD 187	*G-Men: Bootleg Series Volume One* (3-CD box-set, 11/92)
Castle	CLACD 315	*Tattoo* (1/94)
Castle	CLACD 316	*Blueprint* (2/94)
Castle	CLACD 352	*Calling Card* (3/94)
I.R.S	72438 35783 20	*A Blue Day For The Blues* (1995)
Camden	74321 627972	*Etched In Blue* (1998)
Capo	701	*The BBC Sessions* (2-CD set, 1999)
Capo	702	*Let's Go To Work* (4-CD set, 2001)
Capo	703	*Wheels Within Wheels* (2003)
Capo	704	*Meeting With The G-Man+*
Capo	704	*Big Guns: The Very Best Of Rory Gallagher*
EAGCD		*Live At Montreux* (31/7/2006)
Razor Mach 10D		*The Best of Rory Gallagher & Taste* (2/88)
Atlantis	7432178134	*Rory Gallagher Forever* (Greek 2 x CD)

RORY GALLAGHER REMASTERED CDS

CAPO	101	*Rory Gallagher* (1999)
CAPO	102	*Deuce* (1998)
CAPO	103	*Live In Europe* (1999)
CAPO	104	*Blueprint* (2000)
CAPO	105	*Tattoo* (2000)
CAPO	106	*Irish Tour '74* (1998)
CAPO	107	*Against The Grain* (1999)
CAPO	108	*Calling Card* (1998)
CAPO	109	*Photo-Finish* (1998)
CAPO	110	*Top Priority* (1999)
CAPO	111	*Stage Struck* (1999)
CAPO	112	*Jinx* (2000)
CAPO	113	*Defender* (1999)
CAPO	114	*Fresh Evidence* (1998)

RORY GALLAGHER: GUEST APPEARANCES

Blue Horizon STEC125 Mike Vernon: *Bring It Back Home* (1971)

Chess 60013 Muddy Waters: *The London Sessions* (1972)

Mercury 6672 008 Jerry Lee Lewis: *The Session* (1973)

Reading Festival 1973 (1973)

Chess CH60026 Muddy Waters & Howlin' Wolf: *London Revisited* (1974)

RCA/UTOPIA Albert King: *Live 1975* (1977)

Polydor 2383465 Joe O'Donnell: *Gaodhal's Vision* (1977)

CHR 1158 Lonnie Donegan: *Puttin' On The Style* (1978)

EPC/86000 Mike Batt: *Tarot Suite* (1979)

EPIC 25996 Box Of Frogs: *Box Of Frogs* (1984)

Mercury 422 824 652-1 Gary Brooker: *Echoes In The Night* (1985)

Ariola 260 294 The Fureys & Davey Arthur: *The Scattering* (1989)

TARA Davey Spillane Band: *Out Of The Air* (1988)

SHANACHIE 53008 Phil Coulter: *Words And Music* (1989)

DOJO CD243 Stiff Little Fingers: *Flags and Emblems* (1991)

Baycourt RTÉ CD 157-30 The Dubliners: *Thirty Years A-Greying* (1992)

Chris Barber and His Band: *The Outstanding Album 1968–1972* (1993)

SPV 085-89422 Samuel Eddy: *Strangers On The Run* (1995)

Castle TRA CD100 Energy Orchard: *Pain Killer* (1995)

Seagull Peter Green: *Peter Green Songbook*

Peter Green: *Rattlesnake Guitar – The Music of Peter Green* (1995)

ASC 33CD Roberto Manes: *Phoenician Dream*

ACKNOWLEDGEMENTS

One's earliest experience of encouragement is critical. When I was a boy of ten, Dick Condon, a teacher at my school in Raheny, opened up a world of music for me, ranging from Gilbert and Sullivan operettas to classical concerts in St Francis Xavier Hall. Through my teenage years, encouraged by my beloved parents, Brendan and Pauline, I headed for the legendary Grove and early sightings of Sugar Shack, Ditch Cassidy and the News. There was a memorable night in the CYMS in Fairview to hear Gary Moore, Noel 'Nollaig' Bridgeman, Brendan 'The Brush' Shiels and Philip Lynott – Skid Row – in the company of my best pal, Eddie Breslin. It expanded that vista of popular music, with the flame being fanned by Alan Freeman, John Peel and Kid Jensen – a torch later lit here by Larry Gogan, Ken Stewart and Ronan Collins and in the 1970s by Dave Fanning, Bob Harris and Paul Jones. Seeing Taste in the National Boxing Stadium in 1968 was electrifying.

I've worked near music for over forty years, from moving from Polydor in the mid-1970s to the local record industry, working with guitarist and record producer Jerry Hughes, to forming Bus Records with Tony Bradfield in the early 1980s – what a blast! In 1988, I trained as a radio producer with Raidio Telefís Éireann and since then, I've produced a wide range of programming, including music specials, *Bluestime* in the early-1990s and the *Metal Show* on 2FM. The *Bluestime* signature tune on RTÉ Radio 1 was 'Ain't No Saint' by Rory Gallagher. Following Rory Gallagher's untimely death in 1995, I was invited by the distinguished traditional Irish musician Matt Cranitch to give the Inaugural Rory Gallagher Memorial Lecture in the Curtis Auditorium of the then Cork School of Music as part of the Cork Institute of Technology's Arts Festival. Since that time in 1995, the motivation to chart the career of Ireland's first rock star was never far away.

Particular thanks to the Northern connection of John Flanigan, Joe Cohen, Colin McKeown (Eddie Kennedy's nephew) and members of the Northern Ireland Guitar Society; William (Billy) Kennedy, John Wilson, Lou Martin, Gerry McAvoy and Terri Hooley and especially the friendship of the Minister – Dino McGartland – his wife, Annie, and their daughters, Ciara and Nicola.

In Cork: a special thank you to Rory for the music, Louis de Paor for 'Halla na Cathrach', Tony and Monica Moore, Paul Dromey, Pat Conway, Rory Cobbe, Bill O'Brien, Michael Crowley, Sheena Crowley, Eric Kitteringham, Pete Brennan, Mick Daly, The Lee Valley String Band, 'Irish' Jack Lyons, The Lee Delta Blues Club, Cork City Library, Marian Keohane, Joe and Marion O' Herlihy. I'm grateful to Liam Ronayne and good friend Pat Horgan for their guidance and enthusiasm.

In Dublin: Tommy Tighe, Michael Traynor, Pat Egan, the wonderful Dave McHugh and Patricia, Leagues O'Toole, Eddie and Stella Breslin, Frank Murray, and Tony and Irene Bradfield.

In Britain: the late John Coward, Gary Hood, Harry Lees, Jed Thomas, Peter Green, John Pearson, dear friends Mike and Jo Viner, Harry Shapiro, photographer Brian Smith, close friends Gordon and Dorothy Morris in Cumbria for their generosity and support, Chris Eccleshall, filmmaker Tony Palmer, and Michael Gray for great advice.

In Europe: Frank Eichler; '$20 Dollar Bill' Karlheinz Bilstein and Sabine and all the Wiesbaden crew, Ed Erbeck, Klaas and Annette Spijker and all in Leeuwarden, Barry McCabe, those wonderful second-hand vinyl stores in Monastiraki in Athens, Juan Casas Rigall, Dan McCarthy, and Cork City Library for inspiring the Walking Tour of Rory Gallagher's Cork.

In the USA: thank you to Charlie Gili, John Ganjamie and Joyce, Perry and Maryann de Leo.

I appreciate the generosity of spirit of the photographers Colm Henry, Fin Costello, Ed Erbeck, Roy Esmonde, Jo Clauwaert, John Crone, and Anne Kearney in the photographic archive of the *Irish Examiner*.

Thanks to all at The Collins Press for their encouragement and support, with a special word of thanks to my editor and guiding light, Laurence Fenton.

For more than thirty years, my darling wife Helen Roche has had to tolerate my accumulation of vinyl and 1970s rock memorabilia – at last, it all seems to make sense. Love you Heds xxx

INDEX

Note: Numbers in *italic* refer to photo captions

Rory Gallagher Place, Cork. The sculpture, unveiled on 25 October 1997, was designed by Geraldine Creedon, a childhood friend of Rory's (courtesy Paula Elmore).